"Jerry White shares wisdom from a lifetime of leadership. His rules are penetrating, perceptive, and practical. They are valuable whether you're just starting out or wrestling with problems at the top."

—KIRK HUMPHREYS, chairman, The Humphreys Company;
former mayor of Oklahoma City

"Dr. Jerry White literally wrote the book on astronautical engineering that taught me the fundamentals of how to navigate into the heavens aboard the space shuttle. Now he's written a book on how to navigate through life with the same destination in mind. A must-read."

—GENERAL KEVIN CHILTON, USAF, astronaut

"In a day when common sense is amazingly uncommon, Jerry White offers brilliant yet everyday rules to live by. Draw up a chair, sit down with someone who's been there and done that, and take a listen."

—ELISA MORGAN, author of *She Did What She Could*;
publisher, www.fullfill.org; president emerita, MOPS International

"This book presents a commonsense approach to life in a noisy, demanding, and hectic world. Jerry White has the unique ability to show us how to live with peace, joy, and discipline. It's a great tool for helping bring order to one's daily journey."

—MIKE TIMMIS, author of *Between Two Worlds*;
chairman, Prison Fellowship; business owner and CEO

"The rules for life presented in this book are not just words; they have been lived by, tested, and found to be sound. They work! This book is simple yet quite profound, humbly presented by a man who for decades has studied God's Word and honestly tried to live by it."

—MAJOR GENERAL KEN HABEDANK, USAF, retired

"Jerry takes years of leading, teaching, and coaching and puts his best lessons learned into this concise, easy-to-read list of rules to live by. Great advice for young and old."

—RON CAMERON, chairman, Mountaire Corporation

JERRY WHITE

52 PRINCIPLES FOR A BETTER LIFE

RULES TO LIVE BY

NAVPRESS

Discipleship Inside Out™

NAVPRESS
Discipleship Inside Out™

NavPress is the publishing ministry of The Navigators, an international Christian organization and leader in personal spiritual development. NavPress is committed to helping people grow spiritually and enjoy lives of meaning and hope through personal and group resources that are biblically rooted, culturally relevant, and highly practical.

For a free catalog go to www.NavPress.com
or call 1.800.366.7788 in the United States or 1.800.839.4769 in Canada.

ISBN-13: 978-1-60006-270-4

Cover design by Arvid Wallen

Some of the anecdotal illustrations in this book are true to life and are included with the permission of the persons involved. All other illustrations are composites of real situations, and any resemblance to people living or dead is coincidental.

Unless otherwise identified, all Scripture quotations in this publication are taken from the *Holy Bible, New International Version*® (NIV®). Copyright © 1973, 1978, 1984 by International Bible Society. Used by permission of Zondervan. All rights reserved. Other versions used include: the New American Standard Bible® (NASB), Copyright © 1960, 1962, 1963, 1968, 1971, 1972, 1973, 1975, 1977, 1995 by The Lockman Foundation. Used by permission; *THE MESSAGE* (MSG). Copyright © 1993, 1994, 1995, 1996, 2000, 2001, 2002. Used by permission of NavPress Publishing Group; and the *Holy Bible*, New Living Translation (NLT), copyright © 1996, 2004. Used by permission of Tyndale House Publishers, Inc., Wheaton, Illinois 60189. All rights reserved.

Library of Congress Cataloging-in-Publication Data

White, Jerry E., 1937-
  Rules to live by : 52 principles for a better life / Jerry White.
      p. cm.
  Includes bibliographical references.
  ISBN 978-1-60006-270-4
  1. Christian life. I. Title.
  BV4501.3.W46623 2010
  248.4--dc22

                          2010016137

Printed in the United States of America

1 2 3 4 5 6 7 8 / 14 13 12 11 10

CONTENTS

2. RELATIONSHIP RULES

Foreword

I've always been a firm believer in simple truths. As a writer, I like to break down complex and profound ideas into easily understood chunks and then show readers how they can apply those learnings to their daily lives, both at home and on the job.

The book you are holding is a treasure-trove of simple truths from my friend Jerry White—someone who has lived through more of life's ups and downs than most of us. His rational, comforting words are a welcome dose of common sense in these challenging times.

What is interesting to me is that *Rules to Live By* flows along the same lines as our ranked values at The Ken Blanchard Companies. The #1 ranked value at Blanchard is Ethical Behavior, and in this book you will find segments such as *Do What You Say You'll Do, Say "Thank You,"* and *Treat People Well,* which all relate to ethics and character. Our #2 ranked value is Relationships—such an important part of our lives, and right in step with Jerry's chapters on *Don't Get Mad at the Little Things, Make and Keep Close Friends,* and *Don't Carry a Grudge.* Success is our #3 ranked value—because there's nothing wrong with being successful—and the sections titled *Work Hard, Compete, but Don't Be Competitive,* and *Think Long Term* resonate with that value. Finally, Learning is the #4 ranked value at Blanchard—because when you stop learning, you might as well lie down and let them throw dirt on you. The chapters such as *Learn to Concentrate, Read,* and *Learn in Depth—Don't Be Shallow* remind us how important it is to constantly keep learning.

As a firm believer that servant leadership is the only way to get great results *and* human satisfaction, I enjoyed the sections on *Know Yourself, Give Yourself, Be Available, Focus on Contribution, not Position,* and *Avoid Pride and Boastfulness.* Whatever you're interested in, Jerry will have some good thoughts about it.

I think you'll find this to be one of those books you'll keep handy, either on your nightstand or maybe on an end table in your living room. Give it as a gift to your kids, your colleagues, your mail carrier. Read a chapter a week—with fifty-two chapters, this book can guide you through a whole year. Or do what I do: Stick your finger in the book each morning and read whatever page opens up. You may discover a message you can use on that particular day.

Life is a very special occasion. Thanks, Jerry, for caring enough to bring together these important life principles so we can all keep them fresh in our minds.

—Ken Blanchard, coauthor of *The One Minute Manager*®
and *Leading at a Higher Level*

What's Here, and Why

Most of life is spent stumbling around, trying to figure out what to do next. While we're still pondering why our last step went wrong, we stagger forward in the dark with groping hands outstretched, hoping not to run into anything.

Now and then, somewhere along the way, we discover a few things that seem to work for us. We focus on them and close our eyes to other possibilities. Occasionally we learn something from someone else and add that to our list of simple things that work.

Simple. That work. I like that. After all, I'm an engineer. I like things that work, and I like figuring out why they do.

Having been thrust into leadership roles I never imagined, by necessity I've had to stop stumbling so much and learn to do things better (though I still feel I'm faltering at times—I guess that's something that never ends).

For More Freedom

In our hectic and pressured lives, most of us long for less stumbling and more consistency and order. At the same time, we want to be flexible and responsive to the needs of our family, friends, and coworkers. We instinctively resist an overly structured life, at work and personally. We want to live by grace, not legalism. We want freedom, not slavery to systems and agendas. We want proper focus, not more stress.

To do all this, we rustle through self-help books, retool our schedules and priorities, and explore ideas on reinventing ourselves, our marriages, and our families. Sometimes we retreat for times of meditation or withdrawal to get rejuvenated and back on track.

I've tried all these options, and some of them worked for me to a degree. But something else has been more helpful: I've realized that in order to live sensibly, I've developed, pursued, and practiced a set of "rules" that help me respond to life without having to figure out every situation anew as it arises.

Rules are something we all know about from way back. Most of our childhood is spent learning and developing guidelines and regulations (for how to walk, how to eat, not running out into traffic, saying "please" and "thank you," and hundreds of other things) that formulate our patterns for how to get along in life.

Adults need rules also. Those you'll find in this book are the ones that have especially helped me. Some I follow better than others, but each of them helps order my life, giving my mind the freedom to think about deeper life issues.

It's my hope that these rules will help you in the same way.

A Guarantee

As I've reflected on simple things that work and collected them for you in this book, I've recognized that some are big and important, others small and piddly. None of them is life-saving. (Well, a couple of them could be, if you push a bit deeper.)

But I do guarantee two things about them:

1. *These rules are simple.* They're not rocket science (although rocket science happens to be my field of expertise).
2. *These rules work.* I've tried and applied them all, with varying degrees of success. However, they're a lot like ingredients for a cake. You don't line them up on the kitchen counter and say "Abracadabra," then instantly get a cake. No, you have to get to work, mix everything up, and bake it. (My wife, Mary, has finally stopped laughing uncontrollably at the notion that I'd know how to make a cake.)

So that's your task in applying my rules. Dive in, mix them up, try them out. There are fifty-two of them, so you may even want to take one a week for a year and really think about each one and apply it to your life. Or just jump to whatever looks most interesting to you. They're roughly arranged in three parts — (1) "A Better You," (2) "Relationship Rules," and (3) "Enhancing Your Work and Effectiveness" — but there's a lot of overlap, and they all interrelate and support each other.

So put them together in whatever way best fits *you*.

And along the way, have a great read!

A Better You

THINK

Think!

That seems simple enough, doesn't it?

Actually, we're thinking all the time, of course. Our minds work constantly, never stopping. We reason and reflect, we ponder and dream, we plot and plan, we wonder and imagine.

Much of our thinking is uncontrolled and uninitiated, even undirected. After doing something unwise or making a poor decision, you've probably had someone reproach you with these words: "*What* were you *thinking?*"

The truth is, maybe you weren't thinking—at least, not proactively and purposefully. You were just reacting. Or you may have been swept along by some emotional impulse.

A good reminder for us all is to *not* simply react or respond by impulse. Force yourself to actually *think* and to keep a purposeful, controlled thought process moving forward in whatever you're facing or experiencing.

A good foundation for this is to realize the built-in patterns in how you and others process things mentally—your thinking styles. Can you identify yourself in one of the following descriptions?

Analytical thinkers want to gather and sort and analyze all the facts and data before making a decision and acting on it. Those facts can be quite scattered or diverse, but the analytical thinker will make order out of them.

Logical thinkers want everything in order—1, 2, 3, 4, 5, then decide. *Not* 3, 1, 5, 4 . . . Correct sequence and order make these people feel secure. When a step or fact is missing, their inner self wants to delay the decision.

Intuitive thinkers drive the analytical or logical thinker crazy because they sense or intuit their way to a course of action. They read the situation but can't explain reasons or facts for their conclusions. Yet they're often a good judge of people, and they especially excel where facts and data are sparse. Although women may seem to have a corner on this style, many men think this way also.

Creative thinkers see possibilities and opportunities everywhere. They come up with ideas, one after another. Innovation energizes them. Follow-through may be seriously lacking, and many of their ideas may not work anyway, but some will. This thinking style may be segmented—that is, limited to certain areas. Someone may be a creative genius in mathematics but incapable of designing new ways to organize and manage people, or vice versa.

Each of these styles has its place and value. Each can be learned and used by anyone to some extent.

Which one of these is *your* most natural pattern? Which one seems to be the typical style for each of the people you interact with most often?

Learn that well and make the most of it in your own thoughts and in your relationships with others.

2

LEARN TO THINK WELL

To really think *well* is a learned skill. That's the ultimate goal of education. And if we've committed ourselves to being lifelong learners, that will include a continual refinement in how we think. A person who stops learning and stops growing mentally will begin to die.

One of the greatest benefits of my engineering education was learning to think according to the scientific method. In simple form, the pattern is this:

1. State the problem.
2. Gather the relevant facts.
3. Analyze and identify possible solutions to the problem.
4. Test each solution.
5. Choose the best solution and implement it.

That kind of analytical thinking is what some people do naturally, but for most it's a learned skill.

If that five-step pattern isn't a mental process you typically follow when there's a problem to solve or a tough decision to make, try being more intentional about carrying out each of those five stages of thought.

As adults, after our formal education, we learn to think primarily by what we experience, what we read, and what we discover by talking to and listening to others. We then develop experiences that validate or invalidate our thinking. Make sure you're actively engaged in this pattern of thinking activities as you determine to learn to think well.

LEARN TO CONCENTRATE

After two years of hectic work and activity in my Air Force assignment at Cape Kennedy, I realized I was sorely neglecting my family. As we moved to Dayton, Ohio, where I began studies toward a master's degree, I made a strategic decision. I decided to do all my studying at home, where I would be accessible to my children. I decided to always eat dinner with them and play with them in the evening.

In Dayton, we lived in World War II–era housing. In our cluster, about twenty two-story apartments were arranged in a "U" shape. The families living there were all young, with lots of kids — almost a hundred in this cluster. You can imagine the cacophony of noise, especially in the summer when open windows were a necessity (the apartments weren't air-conditioned). It was there that I learned to concentrate. I learned to tune out the noise and focus my attention on studying. Little did I realize how helpful this developed skill would prove to be in the future.

Whether you're in an open office, an airplane, or your home, the ability to ignore noise and disruptions and to focus your mind and energy is valuable.

A second aspect of concentration is to discipline your mind from wandering in the midst of a task. The distraction here is you, not others. This is relatively easy when you're deeply engrossed in something you enjoy. But while doing other necessary tasks, you might often find that your mind wanders, almost randomly, to other things. My solution is simple: Keep a pad of paper handy to record those thoughts and relieve your mind of the distraction and to remind you to deal with it later.

There's a downside to this concentration. You can lose your situational awareness and be too inaccessible to others. I remember my children getting my attention by repeating, "Earth to Dad, Earth to Dad." I needed to unlearn my concentration to some degree. (Today they just blame it on my poor hearing!)

For mothers of young children, this is an almost impossible task, since they must multitask and be alert to everything around them. Even then, learning to focus for short periods is important.

Concentration is a learned skill. It's a discipline of the mind, an act of your will. But it requires practice and decision. To begin, try total concentration for short periods of time—about five minutes. Try focusing first on something you especially enjoy. You can later increase the amount of time as well as tackle more challenging subjects and tasks.

Meanwhile, for those of us who already do this too well, allow yourself to be interrupted. But that's another topic.

LEARN TO RELAX

Much of my life has been spent doing and accomplishing. It was challenging and fulfilling. I was also deeply involved in helping and mentoring young people. For a time, my wife and four children, the most important part of my life, were along for the ride. I was young and really didn't know better. Now, in retrospect, there's much I would change about my lifestyle.

Relaxing and having fun for fun's sake wasn't in my playbook back then. Yes, I played sports of several kinds, but even that had a serious bent to it.

In *Autobiography of a Business Woman*, Alice Foote MacDougall astutely observed that when work "becomes at once a delight and a tyrant," then "even when the time comes and you can relax, you hardly know how." That was me.

Then one day I ran into a brick wall. I burned out and found myself emotionally and physically depleted. This certainly was *not* fun. Part of my path back to full health was learning to relax. That meant changing long-held patterns of thinking and living.

We relax in three areas of our lives: physical, mental, and emotional. And everyone achieves relaxation in a different way. What relaxes me might give you a tension headache!

Physical relaxation is the simplest. It involves downtime, limiting work schedules, getting away for a weekend or a vacation. It also involves physical activities that relax and refresh you: hunting, sports, sewing, gardening, reading, exercising, and so on. It means truly taking time off.

I used to wonder at what seemed to be an overemphasis on the Sabbath in the Old Testament of the Bible. I understand it better now. God has built into our physical makeup a need—even a requirement—for a day each week for rest, play, worship, and change of pace.

Mental relaxation engages your mind in areas of interest apart from your work. For me, that meant reading lighter books. I learned to enjoy the novels of Louis L'Amour. For you it might mean reading a favorite magazine or going to a good movie.

Emotional relaxation is closely linked with both physical and mental relaxation. Worry, anxiety, anger, and resentment are major emotional drains. There's no magic formula for getting around them. Reconciling oneself to what cannot be changed helps relieve us to some extent.

The spiritual dimension of our lives can have a big impact in our emotional being. Begin reading a book that speaks to spiritual issues. Seek out a church that's recommended by people you admire and trust.

Some people feel that relaxation techniques such as yoga or some form of meditation help them. That's usually a temporary fix. The long-term solution requires a lifestyle adjustment.

So learn to relax, because your life depends on it.

5 Be a Loser

Losing gets such a bad rap. Our psyche is geared to trying to be a winner, not a loser.

There's much good to be said about winning, but it's not all it's cracked up to be.

Some people win some endeavors but lose big in the parts of life that really count. They spend everything to win at work — and lose their marriage or children. They win in every competition — and lose their friendships. They win in the big-house, new-car, and new-clothes game — and lose the joy of true satisfaction. They win every argument — and lose relationships and the ability to learn.

Let me give you some ideas of better things to lose:

- *Lose weight.* You'll feel better physically and emotionally.
- *Lose some of your drivenness.* We're all driven in some way — in sports, work, money, politics, success. Your personal

drive is important and valuable but needs moderation.

- *Lose your anger.* No one likes to see you angry, especially your family.
- *Lose your cynicism.* No, everyone's not out to get you. Not even the government or politicians. There are good people out there, and good organizations and programs. Don't make a habit of questioning everything with a raised eyebrow.
- *Lose your prejudices.* Everyone has prejudices. They can be racial, cultural, political, religious, or social. I'm not talking about well-founded beliefs and convictions; being wishy-washy isn't a virtue, but neither is being unreasonably prejudiced. Discovering our prejudice isn't simple, since it resides at such a deep level.
- *Lose your grudges and resentments.* Over the years, we all accumulate grudges over offenses, our upbringing, or perceived mistreatment. You can do little about incidents in the past, so why waste your emotional energy harboring resentment? It will eat on you like cancer. Lose it.
- *Lose arguments.* Especially with your spouse, children, and extended family.
- *Lose your pet peeves.* They don't benefit you.
- *Lose your selfishness.* Looking at your own navel blinds you to the needs of people around you.

6 BE A WINNER

What's this double-talk? After telling you to be a loser, now I'm saying to be a winner?

But these two aren't necessarily contradictory. The key is being sure you're winning the right game.

Where do you always want to be a winner?

- *In your marriage.* If you're married, it's the most important endeavor of your life. If you've been divorced, you know the devastation it causes. Even if you're married and struggling in your satisfaction and happiness, take steps to develop that relationship. Read books on marriage, go to a marriage seminar, see a marriage counselor. One couple we know sees a counselor regularly just for a "tune-up." Build on a good marriage to make it better.
- *With your children.* Time is the big factor that will make you a winner here. Talk with them and listen to them

(and turn off the TV). Go to their concerts and sports events. Make special memories. Eat dinner regularly together.

- *In your friendships.* Learn to develop friendships that have depth and meaning. Be with people you enjoy. Keep the friendships over many years. Find them at church, at work, in your neighborhood, in your hobbies.
- *As a grandparent.* Time passes so rapidly with children and grandchildren. Make time for them. It will reward you and your children. You can make a contribution that no one else can.
- *In your spiritual life.* Life is far more than just existence or the quest for personal fulfillment. Be a searcher for truth and a seeker of God. Examine the life of Jesus in the Bible both as a pattern for your life and for deeper significance of personal belief.

In a world that prefers the focus of winning and glorifies things like sports, the lottery, and entertainment, learn to win in areas of life that truly count and give happiness.

7 ENDURE ADVERSITY

Everyone experiences adversity and difficult times. No one escapes. We don't live in the fairy-tale world of Prince Charming and Cinderella. We live in the real world of conflict, war, financial reverses, relational breakdowns, illness, and suffering.

The real issue in our lives is how we respond to these things.

From Job in the Bible to the Kennedy family, from Abraham Lincoln to scientist Stephen Hawking, from polio-stricken Franklin Roosevelt to prisoner-of-war John McCain, we see many examples of high-achieving men and women whose lives were marked by great adversity.

Our most common and natural responses to adversity are anger, sadness, depression, and resignation. But men and women of character respond with discipline, determination, and a positive attitude. They don't blame others or God. Though the adversity is never welcome, it's accepted and confronted.

I've walked alongside a number of friends battling cancer. They've modeled to me the very best of courage and character. Yes, they experienced fear and even despair at times, but they kept incredibly positive in their actions and outlook, some to the very end. One friend of ours endured a twenty-year battle with cancer. Her life was an inspiration to hundreds and influenced so many to find a deeper spirituality and view of God. Another friend was given eight days to live; yet now, over two years later, he's resolutely facing the future and writing a daily blog that has received more than 100,000 visits.

My early life was influenced by people who faced significant adversity. My mother was divorced in her teens, then raised me in her father's home. She remarried eight years after the divorce and moved 1,500 miles away to begin a new life. In reflection, I realize the courage it took for her to keep going.

In my teen years, I was impacted by a young businessman who had cerebral palsy. I worked in his printing business and sat under his teaching in church. He remained my friend for all his life. The courage and determination I saw in him caused me to see that many of my own difficulties were minor. His positive attitude was absolutely remarkable.

Later, when our only son was murdered, Mary and I faced adversity of a depth we'd never known. That story is told in the book Mary wrote called *Harsh Grief, Gentle Hope*.

I've learned that adversity both toughens us and softens us. It toughens us to endure more than we ever thought we could. It softens us to be so much more aware of the adversity of others.

Adversity challenges and deepens my view of God and the spiritual dimensions of life. It has brought me face-to-face with what really matters in life—and it wasn't success and accomplishments, of which I'd experienced more than my share. Adversity put my life in perspective, both humbling me and strengthening me. Because of adversity, I'm no longer the same person but rather I've found a deeper and more lasting satisfaction in life, work, and family.

Don't seek adversity. But when it comes (as it inevitably will), welcome it. Let it drive you to a deeper meaning of life.

Know
Yourself

In my younger years, I wanted to be able to do every-thing—and to do it all well. I was fearful of failure or of looking bad. I kept meeting people of incredible ability or spirituality, and I envied them. I wanted to know language as well as my wife did and have the professional insights of my colleagues Roger and Ed in the field of astrodynamics. I wanted to sing well, play sports well, and be an ideal husband and father. Whatever there was to be or do, I wanted to excel in it.

Perhaps that's a phase most of us go through in our youth. Whether it was a mixture of pride, ego, and ambition, I don't know. To me, it was a normal desire: *to be somebody* and *to accomplish something* in my life.

But soon I began to realize I was quite average in most areas, and it humbled me. In fact, I had to admit I wasn't at all gifted in some skills. For example, although I wanted to be intellectual and be respected for my cool, analytical thinking, I found that my manner of thinking was more emotional and less objective than I would have liked to admit.

When I first came to teach astronautics at the Air Force Academy, our faculty dean told the new instructors, "Remember, just because you're an expert at one thing doesn't make you an expert on everything." That was a timely caution.

I've come to realize that while I'm interested in history, economics, and many other disciplines, I'm not well educated in them. I can continue to read and learn in a given field, but that won't make me an expert. The knowledge explosion in the recent decades means that no one can be a specialist in more than one or two areas.

But I was also encouraged to find there were some things I could do well (such as teaching and leading), and others that I could do fairly well by using hard work to make up for my lack of skill.

You'll always find others who have better abilities than you have (or think you have), and it can tempt you to envy. But when you *know yourself,* you'll be more content with the way God made you and with your lot in life. Looking realistically at myself through the eyes of reality, experience, and my closest friends, I find I'm far more content and at peace with myself and how I'm made.

In this process, I've been guided by these words from the Bible: "Be honest in your evaluation of yourselves, measuring yourselves by the faith God has given us."[1] God wants us to know ourselves and know that whatever gifts and abilities we have are from Him.

This doesn't mean we should refuse to do tasks for which we're not particularly gifted. We often must act outside our gifting just because a task needs to be accomplished. I may need to fix a bicycle for my children whether or not I'm good at it. Or I may need to lead or organize activities even if my gift is serving, not leadership. But I shouldn't make such tasks my main focus. We do what we must, but when we have options, we should work with what we do well.

9 READ

Someone has said that if you can read yet choose not to, you're really no better off than someone who's illiterate.

In ancient times, the elite were the only ones who could read and write, and they controlled the destiny of nations. Even today, the world continues to be divided between those who are literate and those who are not, although a remarkable percentage of people today can read.

Yet a large number of them don't read beyond what they must to keep their jobs.

Reading is one of the most valuable skills you can develop and practice. It takes you to worlds you've never seen. It plants ideas and concepts that can revolutionize your life. It will develop you as a mature, thoughtful person. It will challenge your prejudices. I think it's an absolute necessity for personal growth.

Reading requires discipline and skill, both in choosing what to read and in reading it. This skill is developed primarily by practice. You may need a dictionary at your side to help you understand what you're reading. Also, reading out loud can be a good exercise to develop your skill.

Many people don't read well. Recently I was leading a group discussion on the Bible and asked a person to read a paragraph. He asked not to. Later he told me he had a learning disability and found it difficult to read, especially in the morning. Another man told me he finally admitted to himself that he couldn't read so he decided to learn. He sought out a kindergarten teacher and asked her to tutor him. That took courage and determination.

Do whatever you need to do to learn to read better.

I read slowly, but I still keep reading. Here are my suggestions on what to read daily:

- The Bible
- A newspaper (read at least one article fully) or Internet news service
- Part of some book

Set a goal to complete a book a month on average—you'll never regret doing this. I recommend choosing and reading books regularly in these categories:

- Something related to your work
- A book on a spiritual subject

- A book in an area of personal interest (your hobby, history, politics, and so on)
- A book in a new area for you
- Some fiction (I read escapist novels)

Some useful rules for reading:

- Don't hesitate to read two or three books at a time. I usually keep several active for a change of pace.
- You don't need to finish everything you start. If a book doesn't capture your interest after a few chapters, just skim the rest and go on to something else.
- Read some books completely, especially if it's on a subject you feel a need to understand.

READ THE BIBLE

No one's education can be complete without reading the best-selling and most widely distributed book of all time: the Bible. In recent centuries it has become increasingly accessible to people in all walks of life in nearly every language.

Most people in the Western world own at least one copy of it and know at least bits and pieces of the story it tells. But not many have read it thoroughly or really grappled with its moral and spiritual teachings.

It's often described as great literature, which it is. It contains unsurpassed poetry and song and timeless classics of both storytelling and philosophical discourse. But it's far more than all that. It has captured and motivated the hearts of nobles and peasants, soldiers and servants, scholars and shopkeepers throughout the centuries. It baffles the intellect of geniuses and soothes the soul of the simple and uneducated. It's personal yet sweeps the boundaries of history of countries and continents. It speaks of the destiny of nations.

It is quoted often but also misquoted. It's often misunderstood and misused. It gives brilliant guidance yet is perverted for evil when portions of it are taken out of context.

Certainly it's a deeply spiritual and religious book, portraying the epic story of the Jewish people as well as the life of Jesus and the adventures and experiences of His followers. It also contains moral and leadership principles, plus abundant teaching on the family, work, and wealth. It instructs us in our relationships with one another and in law and government. It teaches compassion for the poor and destitute. It gives women rights and status that were granted nowhere else in the ancient world.

It exposes evil and wickedness and shows the folly of pride and arrogance. It never hides the foibles and shortcomings of its heroes.

And, of course, it puts forth a Savior of the world and of individuals.

We devour books on our work, our health, our wealth, our relationships, and our happiness. Yet here's one book that addresses all these topics. We owe it to ourselves to include it in our habits of reading. Some go to churches or synagogues and hear about it. But we need to experience its message directly, in the quietness of our own home.

Let me suggest a simple plan:

1. Buy a paperbound edition of the Bible in a modern translation, printed in a type size that's easily read.

2. Read one chapter a day from both the Old Testament and the New Testament. If you sometimes wish to read more, fine, but don't be driven. Keep a leisurely, unrushed pace.

3. Use a marker or pen to highlight important words, phrases, and sentences and to write your questions in the margins.

4. Circle one or two key words or thoughts each day to reflect on.

5. Enjoy reading it. Don't try to put everything together at once. Get the sweep of the story.

Regardless of where you are in your spiritual journey, you'll find yourself stimulated and refreshed. At times you'll be puzzled with the "whys" of the account. The Bible will raise questions in your mind even as it instructs you in life issues.

Over time you'll be surprised at what you learn, at how misconceptions are clarified, and at how facts of history begin to line up. This will begin to impact your life and relationships. And, yes, it will also make you uncomfortable at times as you begin to measure your actions by what the Bible teaches.

Maybe that's why many avoid reading this book, fearing it may open life doors they wanted to keep closed. But I've found my time spent in Bible reading to be the most refreshing, consistently satisfying activity of my life.

So give it a try. Stay with it at least a month; then you'll know if you want to keep going.

11 Write Something Every Day

Few people—especially men—ever write down what they're thinking. But the most successful people write things out: their thoughts, plans, to-do lists, reflections on the past, and plans and dreams for the future. It helps them focus.

I like these words attributed to E. L. Doctorow: "Writing is an exploration. You start from nothing and learn as you go." He also said, "Writing is a socially acceptable form of schizophrenia."

Especially in times of distress and difficulty, our thoughts become a jumbled mass of entangled threads. Only when we start writing them out do the impulses and mixed-up logic begin to sort out. Writing forces us to think more clearly.

Particularly when you're trying to make a major life decision, writing down the pros and cons will help clarify the issues. Also record any counsel that other people have given you about the decision. This helps you be more objective.

Writing is also a wonderful way to record and preserve events, joys, victories, and good times. We so quickly forget details in the past as they're overcome by time and today's events, so I recommend that you write something every day by way of a personal journal or reflection.

Not long ago, we gave our twelve-year-old granddaughter a blank journal. She immediately began to record her thoughts.

You can write with pen on paper in an actual journal, or you can keyboard it into a file on your computer. For years I wrote on paper, but my terrible penmanship drove me to the computer.

Here are some ideas of what and how to write in your journal.

- Keep it simple. Don't get too complicated or overly careful. Just let it flow.
- List the day's happenings and facts, starting with the weather.
- Write at least one sentence on how you feel about something that happened: your daughter's birthday, meeting another parent at a school function, your golf score, or a call from your favorite uncle or aunt.
- Use names and facts.
- Jot down a prayer or a thought.
- Note any memorable conversations.

It's important to write *for yourself.* No one else need ever read your journal.

For me, the contents of my daily journal entry are simple:

- The date, day of week, and time
- Something on the weather
- A short review of yesterday
- A thought from my daily Bible reading (since I usually start my day with that)
- A note on issues I'm facing or concerns I have

Your total entry may be just a few lines. At times it may be longer. A sample entry might be:

January 5. Thursday, 7 a.m.
Weather: cloudy, 28 degrees.

My Bible reading was Psalm 100. I was reminded to be thankful.

Yesterday was a disaster. Nothing went quite like I planned. But I did get most of the projects at work done. Frankly, in this economy I worry about my job. Probably nothing to worry about. But with Jack in college, finances are tight.

Had a great time at Hannah's basketball game. They won 43–28. She played well. What a pleasure to see her growing up. I could not be more proud.

Not exactly Shakespeare, is it?

After you get the hang of it, venture into a bit more reflection.

As you grow more comfortable with it, who knows? Someday you might write your autobiography—for an audience that includes at least your children and grandchildren.

12 REMEMBER YOUR PAST

The town sat like a postage stamp in the middle of a green carpet of Iowa farmland — corn, oats, and soybeans. It was two blocks long east to west, and two blocks wide north to south. Three street lights hung by wobbly wires crossed Main Street, which had no sign because everyone knew it was Main Street.

Our house, the oldest in town, was on the east side, only fifty feet from the tracks of the Rock Island Railroad. The house shook in a comforting way whenever a train roared through town, especially the twice-a-day Rock Island Rocket, which sped through at sixty miles per hour. I waited and watched with wonder and amazement. I remember when I was very young my family keeping me from getting very close to it.

Grandpa Tony and Grandma Christina lived in that square Iowa house with three sons, two daughters, and me (the son of their youngest daughter, Lois).

It was a great place to grow up. I had the run of the town, a cookie at every kitchen door. But it wasn't always fun for everyone else.

Mother had borne me at age seventeen, dropping out of high school. She and my father moved in with her parents, but that didn't work out for my father. Grandma was demanding of everyone. My parents' marriage blew up, and my father left in anger. I was only a few months old. The divorce soon followed. I still know little more than that about my parents' breakup; in good Norwegian fashion, no one in my mother's family ever—and I mean *ever*—talked about it.

Then all hell broke loose. After America entered World War II, my oldest two uncles were drafted into the army. Like all the other young men in the town and from nearby farms, they went off to war.

The next year, Grandma Christina died. I remember creeping into the living room, peeking into the casket. I'd never seen a dead person before. I don't remember crying; perhaps I did.

For Grandpa Tony, it seemed as if his world were falling apart. His wife was dead, his oldest sons were at war, his younger daughter was divorced. I became the center of his world, and I loved him dearly.

As the war dragged on, my memories were of Grandpa every night with his ear glued to the wooden, curved-top radio tuned to station WHO in Des Moines, listening to war news. His mind was never off his sons, worry and anxiety gripping him. It caused him to start drinking too much, though I didn't understand this at the time.

My one-room schoolhouse had a wonderful teacher. The two other kids my age, a boy and a girl, were my friends. It was an idyllic time for me. I knew or felt nothing of the wrenching world events or the deep pain of the adults around me.

In the last year of the war, my mother met a man who was home on furlough from the Army Air Corps. She fell in love, and they were married. Then he went back to the war in the Far East.

When peace finally came in 1945, both my uncles returned, as did my new stepfather. Then my life was turned upside down. I left that small town and my beloved grandfather; I joined my mother and a father I didn't know, traveling 1,500 miles west to Spokane, Washington, a city of 150,000 people at that time.

Those are my roots, for good or for bad.

In one fascinating statement in the Bible, a prophet of God says, "Look to the rock from which you were cut and to the quarry from which you were hewn."[2] In other words, remember your roots.

All of us have such a history, a set of memories. For some, the story is wonderful, marked by stability, love, and nurturing. For others, the story is painful and disturbing, and the memories still affect you.

We don't have control over the early part of our personal history. We're either cursed or blessed by the events over which we had no say. In our family backgrounds, there are good marriages and bad marriages, good parenting and bad parenting, good experiences and bad experiences. We may recall a childhood filled with love, fun, and warm relationships with extended family. But even in the best of families, there may also be abuse, fear, and sorrow.

All these are part of a past we cannot change. Our pasts underlie much of who and what we are today, all in the higher plan and purposes of God. In biblical terms, this is called the sovereignty of God.

Reflect on your past. Write it down. But please don't blame today on your past. Don't castigate your parents or your siblings to explain things you don't like about yourself or your situation today. Yes, by all means, gain understanding and learn what has formed your personality, your drive, your skills, and your intelligence—even your emotions. But be thankful for your parents. Be grateful for your blessings. Give thanks and credit for all your opportunities, and even for what you don't particularly like about your past. For only when you face those realities can you grow into a better, more mature person. Live today to the fullest with deep gratitude for that which formed you.

On the other hand, if you use your history to excuse your current faults and weaknesses, you'll turn inward, lose your joy, and become a prisoner of your past.

Looking back, I can see that by moving from Iowa to Spokane, I was being introduced to a new life and a wonderful future. At the time, the transition was painful, yet today I'm grateful for it. I'm not sure I would ever have gone to college if I had stayed in that little Iowa town. My difficulties propelled me into a future beyond my wildest imagination.

Allow your history to bless you as mine has done for me.

THINK LONG TERM

13

Most of us live moment by moment and day by day. Life is pressured and hectic, driving us into survival mode.

One of our greatest needs is to think and act long term. We see this, for example, in the matter of savings and retirement planning. It's not quite so obvious in other arenas of life. Let me suggest a few critical areas where I've discovered—often by hard experience—that long-term thinking is imperative.

Your marriage. Take the time and effort to build your relationship with your wife or husband for the long term. With so many marriages ending in divorce, the pain and suffering to couples and to their children is incalculable. Don't let it happen to you. Go to a marriage seminar. Read marriage books. See a marriage counselor. Be on the same page spiritually with your spouse. Don't allow conflict and arguments to remain unresolved. Build your marriage to last for the long haul.

Your children. Time with your children is much shorter than you imagine. Those babies are soon graduating from high school and college. So invest your time in them; be a part of their activities, listen to them, and help guide them morally and spiritually in the right directions. Protect them and encourage them. Take the time! Learn how to be a better parent. Read Tim Kimmel's *Grace-Based Parenting* or another highly regarded parenting book.

Your health. Many of us don't get serious about our health until something goes wrong: cancer, diabetes, high blood pressure, or just the aches of getting older. Guard your health with adequate exercise, proper nutrition, weight control, and regular medical checkups. Don't allow your body and mind to be enslaved and damaged by stress or alcohol or drugs.

Your money. There are hundreds of books and resources to help you be wise in setting and achieving long-term financial goals. My one piece of advice in this area is this: Avoid debt like the plague.

Your skills. The world of work is changing so that many of today's valued skills may not be relevant in a few years. Always work on developing your professional or job skills. Prepare for something different, even if you're at or nearing retirement age. Go back to school, take courses online, attend seminars or skills workshops. Don't grow stale or complacent.

Long-term thinking and planning will always make you better prepared for the future, even when surprises come that you never imagined.

WASTE TIME

I've spent much of my life being proactive, busy, organized, focused, and (some would say) driven. While on vacation, I might look back at the end of a day and lament, "I really didn't accomplish anything today." Mary then chides me for thinking that way, but it seems I can't help myself. Years of practice makes me want to always be accomplishing something.

At times I've gone away somewhere on a personal retreat to give my time to writing or studying, but I found that I was too wound up to do any good writing or study well. In order to free up my mind to begin probing outside my regular routines and responsibilities, I learned I first had to "do nothing"—to occupy myself in leisure reading, naps, walks, or recreation.

Often while doing these things, I felt as though I were wasting time. Yet the reality was that they did far more for my work and life than I ever expected. They refreshed and rejuvenated me. They took my mind to other realms of thought. They made me realize that I'm not the center of the universe, or even the center of my work. They brought in new perspectives on problems and opportunities.

Take time to sit and do nothing. Look up at the sky and observe the movements of clouds. Play with the kids. Take a leisurely stroll somewhere. Read some enjoyable fiction. Indulge in a favorite hobby. Sit with your teenagers and watch TV or a movie together. Play a sport. Plenty of other "time wasters" will come to your mind as you think about it.

We can't make a profession of time wasting. But we can't do without it either.

Is it possible to go too far in wasting time? Of course. Excessive television viewing is especially common. That kind of inactivity leads to indolence. But we all need periodic interruptions of the clamor of life—when we can back away briefly and do things we enjoy that have no other particular purpose.

LET MAGAZINES SIT FOR TWO WEEKS

I learned this rule by accident. Because of my frequent travel in my job, I often found that magazines and mail would pile up. Sometimes my first opportunity to look at them was when they were two to three weeks old. They mostly had "old news" that I'd gleaned through other sources and no longer needed to read. I also discovered that, with the exception of a few articles, I didn't need either the extensive details of the current news or the normally slanted perspective of the reporter.

So even if you can read your magazines the same day they're delivered in the mail, let them sit for a couple of weeks or even months. You'll save hours and be better able to glean what really interests you or what you really need to know.

I found that a ten-minute perusal of the daily newspapers is quite sufficient to inform me satisfactorily. The three-minute "on the hour" radio news is also ample and efficient.

And TV news? Forget it! It's so selective that it's virtually useless. While saying this, I must admit to getting hooked on televised political coverage at times. When I do, I know I'm indulging myself. That's okay; that's my choice.

KEEP PHYSICALLY FIT

Our culture today places an incredible emphasis on health, diet, and fitness. And if you grew up with a religious background, you're probably familiar with the biblical principle that your body is a temple of God and ought to be treated with care. Yet most people today are still overweight and out of shape.

We've heard about the dangers of tobacco, drugs, and alcohol. Clearly they're detrimental. But the failure to keep physically fit is perhaps our most blatant and recurrent sin against our bodies.

Keeping fit is really quite simple. It involves four primary tasks:

- Eat well. (More on this one in the next chapter.)
- Get adequate rest, relaxation, and recreation.
- Exercise moderately.

- Take care of yourself medically (including regular medical checkups and tests and acting responsibly on the results).

I want to say more right here about that third item, exercise. I'm neither a medical doctor nor a fitness expert, but I've researched this subject for myself using several good books. Most experts agree that the goal in exercise includes three things: cardiovascular health, flexibility, and muscle strength.

All three take effort to achieve. Even if you work at a job that requires physical labor, it probably doesn't exercise your heart or increase your flexibility significantly.

Although I applaud those who are really into strenuous exercise, I'm not saying everyone should start training to run marathons, lift weights like Atlas, or achieve washboard abs. Nor do you need to become handball crazy, like I am. Actually, the process for achieving all three exercise goals—a healthy heart, flexibility, and muscle strength—can be summed up in two simple words: *Keep moving*. Regular, brisk walking three to five times a week has been shown to be as beneficial as jogging. The key is to get your heart rate up above a minimal rate (many exercise books can help you calculate that according to your age) over a period of about twenty-five to fifty minutes. This will also work on your flexibility and muscle system.

Along with these walks, I suggest adding stretching and a modest workout with weights.

What are the benefits of such a routine? You'll feel better, sleep better, be healthier, and have more energy—all of which are especially important as you grow older. You'll be able to stay more active than you ever imagined.

I suggest two books to help you in this: *Younger Next Year*, by Chris Crowley and Dr. Henry S. Lodge (Workman Publishing, 2005), and *Power of 10*, by Adam Zickerman and Bill Schley (HarperCollins, 2003).

17

EAT RIGHT

You've seen the svelte woman and the grossly muscular man in advertisements for miracle-working exercise equipment. Did you notice they also appear in the diet ads? *Lose 40 pounds in 30 days! Live longer! Wipe out cancer! Just buy this newly discovered supplement made exclusively from the roots of some exotic shrub in the jungles of the Amazon. It will replace those dangerous fat grams from your favorite fast-food restaurant. Then you can eat what you want and still lose weight.*

You laugh when you encounter those claims, but you also listen (at least I do) and wonder if the product just might work. I must admit I've even ordered a couple of them.

But the real answer for staying trim is so simple: *Eat right.*

Okay, you already know that, so why dwell on it? You aren't planning to get your picture in *Muscle* magazine or *Vogue*. Besides, some people are slender and still unhealthy.

And don't our genes play a big part? Some people eat

voraciously and never add a pound, while others just seem to gain weight almost effortlessly.

On the other hand, being fat neither makes you feel good about yourself nor brings respect from others (in our culture, anyway). Plus, it has often been linked to many health problems.

If you're overweight, you owe it to yourself and your family to learn to eat in a healthier way.

Besides eventually losing weight, there are many other good reasons to eat right:

- You'll feel better.
- You'll see yourself in a more positive light.
- You'll enjoy life more.
- Your relationships will be better.
- You'll heal yourself of many of your illnesses.

There are hundreds of books on the market by qualified experts who can help you eat better. Meanwhile, here's some things I suggest:

- Decide to do something about your eating habits.
- Decide to change your lifestyle.
- Eat smaller portions.
- Eat your veggies.
- Stop eating at fast-food places.
- Curb the chips, beer, and pizza habit.

- Do moderate exercise, especially walking.
- Develop a monthly plan with realistic goals for your weight loss and overall health profile. You'll soon know if such a plan is helping you.

You may feel like telling me, "Don't be such a nag!" But, really, a program like this will work. I've experienced it, and I've seen it work for others.

Don't wait until a major health issue forces you to change your eating habits. Decide to change them *now*.

Don't you feel better already?

FORGET

A "senior moment" isn't something only seniors experience. Everyone at one time or another has forgotten names, places, dates, or events.

Forgetting is actually an important mental function. Our brain is a marvelous creation of God—a massive computer storing every conscious event of our life as we see and hear it. Through a systematic filing process, it relays memories in and out of our conscious awareness. The things we remember most easily are the memories that keep getting rehearsed in our quiet moments, our half-asleep wakefulness at night, or our repeated story grid.

Some memories we can control, some we can't. Even when we wish to erase something from our memory—such as a traumatic experience—it stays indelibly engraved in the reservoirs of our minds.

Our peace of mind has much to do with feelings and emotions

that emerge from these memories. We can actually choose to forget many things that disturb our peace of mind, although this isn't always easy. Yet it is our choice.

Consider these few suggestions of what to forget.

Forget offenses against you. When we constantly remember and rehearse someone's offense against us, it's like continually tearing off a scab so that the wound never heals. That's why the old saying "Don't get mad, get even" is terrible advice. It doubles the hurt and pain for yourself and others. It glorifies hate and diminishes love. It's especially destructive in marriage and in family and personal relationships. It destroys many families and friendships.

Clara Barton, the founder of the American Red Cross, was once asked about a particular offense against her in years past. She replied, "I distinctly remember forgetting that incident." Forgetting can be an act of the will, even though it may not be easy. Even if you can't forget something entirely, you can decide not to allow it to control your thoughts, attitudes, and actions.

This is crucially important because life is filled with offenses large and small. If you allow these to pile up in your mind, their presence will control more and more of your life, robbing it of joy and peace. Why be enslaved by events you can never change?

Forget praise. Be careful not to believe all of your own "press clippings." Accept praise with gratitude and humility, but don't pay too much attention to it, since having a balanced assessment of yourself is far more important than people's opinions.

Forget your prejudices. Deep within us, we all harbor prejudices that come from our family backgrounds, education, and experiences. Our prejudice targets many factors: race, gender, age, education, appearance, wealth, religion, and national origins. Prejudice belittles ourselves and diminishes others. It's one of the most destructive of emotions.

I'm not free or guiltless in this area. Almost daily I sense having feelings toward others that belie my desire to the contrary. But I don't allow the feelings to remain in my thoughts or control my actions.

You can make that same decision.

19

BE QUIET

Knowing when to be quiet is a greater virtue than being an incessant talker, no matter how witty or articulate you may be.

Being a good conversationalist is important, but a key element to that is being a good listener—and you can't listen if you're talking. Being quiet allows others to speak. This is especially true in your family with your spouse and children. Learn to listen and to ask helpful questions that don't provoke defensiveness.

Often, to be a good listener in a conversation necessitates allowing for some moments of total silence. Most of us have a problem waiting more than fifteen seconds (time it!) with no one speaking in a conversation. But those seconds of silence are often what less outgoing people need to feel free to speak freely.

So learn when and how to be quiet in your conversations. For some, that will be easy; for others, it will take a great effort. But the advantages for all include these:

- You'll listen to others better.
- Others will be more drawn to you.
- You'll learn more.
- When you do speak, people will listen more.

And when you're far away from conversations and other people, there's also an *inner* quietness that's important to cultivate. We need times to simply sit or walk and be quiet—not reading or watching TV or listening to the radio or making lists, but just being quiet. You can sit, walk, or lie down. The key is exercising the discipline of silence. Let your mind go many directions. Keep a notepad to jot ideas that flood in.

Even though this practice of silence and solitude is largely lost on our society, executive coaches have caught on to the idea. They suggest a fifteen-minute quiet time before beginning the day's work, or a weekly hour or two with no interruptions.

Over the centuries, religious teachers have advocated a more contemplative lifestyle, and meditation and yoga as stress relievers have often been emphasized in our modern-day world. I'm not advocating a particular method or style but simply stating that we need to learn to be quiet by ourselves. We need quiet time daily for shorter times and periodically for longer times, an hour or two.

I often combine times of inner quietness with reading the Bible or praying, but the silence I'm suggesting is actually a separate and distinctive element.

The advantages of learning to be quiet by yourself include these:

- You'll relax.
- You'll be refreshed.
- Your stress level will go down.
- Your mind will be more creative.
- You'll be healthier.

Blaise Pascal said, "All men's miseries derive from not being able to sit in a quiet room alone." Make sure you're not bringing misery into your life by not possessing and developing the skills of silence and solitude.

GET MAD AT THE RIGHT THINGS

William Wilberforce was an angry man. He saw the injustice and inhumanity of slavery and gave much of his adult life to see it stopped. In the 1780s, as he came to realize the horrors of this terrible institution, he used his position as a member of the British parliament in a long campaign to abolish slavery in the British Empire.

After years of work, a partial victory came in 1807 when Parliament agreed to halt the slave trade. On that occasion, as a speech of tribute to Wilberforce was given and the members of Parliament stood and cheered him, tears streamed down his face.

Yet slavery itself had not been ended. Wilberforce continued to work for this higher goal, but he was often thwarted. The campaign continued for decades, even after the aging Wilberforce was forced to resign from Parliament due to ill health.

Finally, on a late July day in 1833, Wilberforce heard that crucial concessions had been made by the government that

71

would guarantee the passing of a bill to abolish slavery in the empire. Wilberforce died three days later. The bill went through the final stages of approval the following month.

In the attack on injustice, there's much to get angry about: the crime that invades our cities, the plague of drugs that destroys our youth, the injustice of governments in much of the world, the helplessness of the poor, and the rings of prostitutes that use children and teens in almost every country. If we're to become angry and incensed, these are the kinds of issues that should consume us.

The Bible includes classic accounts of those who became angry. Moses threw the first tablets of the Ten Commandments to the ground when he saw the immorality and unfaithfulness of the people of Israel. Jesus became incensed at those who set up shop in Jerusalem's temple to make a profit from the sale of animals for sacrifice; He overturned their tables and drove them out of the temple with a whip.

The Bible says, "Be angry, and yet do not sin."[3] There is a righteous anger. There are larger stakes than simple offenses and preferences; there are causes that are truly worth the investment of your emotions.

What parent wouldn't justifiably become angry at the rape of a daughter or the sale of drugs to a preteen son? But even that anger can consume and destroy you if it isn't focused on the right issues. An example of the right focus is the organization Mothers Against Drunk Drivers. They've educated us all to the societal issues of alcohol and drugs, resulting in tougher laws and penalties.

"The world needs anger," Bede Jarrett writes in *The House of Gold*. "The world often continues to allow evil because it isn't angry enough."

Aristotle said, "Anyone can become angry—that is easy. But to be angry with the right person, to the right degree, at the right time, for the right purpose, and in the right way; this is not easy."

In 1990, our son was brutally and senselessly murdered in a random crime. His assailant, later convicted and imprisoned, was a poverty-stricken drug addict. We could have spent the rest of our lives hating and angry. Instead we chose to speak out on some of the root causes—the violence in our society and the easy access of weapons in our country—without making a campaign of it. Our stand caused some of our friends to be upset with us, yet we had to focus our anger and sorrow in what we felt was the right place.

Are you aware of issues that are worth your anger?

Getting mad can serve a useful purpose. Even though excessive anger can consume you and make you act irrationally, directed anger can focus your emotions and your actions.

We *should* be angry . . .

- when drug dealers are entrapping our children and society in their incredibly destructive habit.

- when we see injustice in our city, nation, or world.
- at the corruption that resides in so much of the developing world, leading to genocide, hunger, and poverty.
- when older kids bully younger children and threaten them in our neighborhoods and schools.
- when older people are treated badly, when the helpless are cheated, or when people are discriminated against.
- that millions of babies are aborted.
- at the glut of child prostitution around the world.

People can make a difference when they focus and band together, harnessing their anger into useful and effective activism. We don't want to be passive and complacent in these important arenas, nor do we want to just complain and bellyache.

Have you come forward to counter injustice when you've had the opportunity? When issues of injustice or evil come your way, don't just run off half-cocked and smash your way forward. Give it careful thought. Join with others who share your passion. Look for long-term solutions, not just temporary corrections.

It's not the emotional and irrational outbursts that are helpful. Rather, our anger should focus our efforts to . . .

- organize to correct a wrong.
- confront a situation or system in a way that brings about change.
- get involved with others in combating an issue.

- use legal or lawful means of countering injustice.
- be certain our facts are correct and that action is justified.
- recruit help in areas beyond our expertise.

Above all, start where you live: your neighborhood, your city, your sphere of influence.

Use your anger—along with patience, wisdom, and persistence—for the right causes. Get mad at something worth your emotions.

21

Don't Get Mad at the Little Things

Your eyes flash. Your stomach churns. Your face flushes over. Your mouth hardens in a line. Your tongue lashes out.

Familiar? Of course. We recognize the signs and emotions of anger welling up inside us. But seldom is it worth the cost we pay: broken relationships, crushed spirits, stress on our hearts, hours required for repair and reconciliation, and much more.

Anger is one of the most destructive forces in life. It leads to divisions, family separation, and destroyed relationships.

No one likes an angry person, especially one whose anger is unpredictable, unjustified, and arising from trivial matters.

Most likely you're not an angry person, but it's very likely that you become angry far more than you should or would like. And it's often triggered by small irritations or offenses.

Anger comes in three stages: an event, the internal response, then the external expression. Why do we get angry? Small children help us see the answer, as they rarely suppress their reactions. When they cry, get mad, hit people, throw things, and say harsh things, what causes these outbursts?

- They're not getting their way.
- Their feelings are hurt.
- They're disappointed.
- They're selfish.
- They're being disciplined.

The same brings on anger in adults:

- We don't get our way (someone cuts us off in traffic, changes channels on the TV program we're watching, or interrupts our schedule).
- Someone offends us or puts us down.
- We have disappointments (at work, in sports).
- Someone intrudes into our personal space or time.
- We're confronted with a need to change or improve something in our lives.

In most cases, these are little things—trivial issues.

What can you do to control your anger and stop wasting an expenditure of emotional energy that causes more trouble than it's worth?

1. *Identify your "hot spots."* I know some of mine. I don't like to be corrected by Mary, especially regarding some of my messy

habits. And I get irritated when people don't do what I say they should do: meet a deadline, come to a meeting, perform a task, keep an appointment. We each have our flash points, our points of irritation. Identify yours.

2. *Recognize your inner responses and emotions.* No one can escape his or her gut response to irritating or angering situations. You feel it in the inner part of you that's almost impossible to control, a feeling that's impossible to deny. For some, it's a slow burn of anger or irritation; for others, it's more explosive.

Whether you express it or stuff it, you know that unmistakable feeling. That feeling is the Creator's alarm system in our inner lives. Just like the well-known "fight or flight" rush of adrenaline in an emergency, this "burn and boil" feeling takes on a life of its own. It causes us to bypass rational thinking and just react. Even when it's not expressed, it becomes the seedbed of stress and resentment that begins to impact our attitudes and actions.

The classic target of these emotions is other drivers when we're out on the highway. But the real target is often our spouses, children, and coworkers—the people we love and need the most.

We have little trouble recognizing the emotions. The challenge is to change and channel them.

3. *Curb the external explosion.* We've all experienced the short circuit between emotions and expression. Before we even think, harsh or angry words spill out of our mouths. It surfaces most often in "safe" places: when we're with family or friends. Here our words of anger maim and wound those dearest to us,

causing often irreparable damage to the relationships. Younger children will often rebound quickly, but older children can be marked for a lifetime as they remember and reexperience your anger. The same can happen in our marriages. In the workplace, such an expression of anger may even cost you your job, or at least damage your credibility and influence.

The solution is remarkably simple: *Strike at the roots.* Use your inner emotional responses as a signal to turn off the switch that lets anger grow or leads to verbal outbursts. We can turn off that switch simply by recognizing the emotion for what it is and not allowing it to persist.

Ask yourself a few easy questions:

- *Why* am I reacting?
- Is it reasonable?
- Is the incident worth the inner stress?

You'll be surprised how often that brief questioning can shut down the emotional inner reaction.

For some, inner reactions of anger are so ingrained and habitual that it's not so easily controlled. In that case, you need a close friend or counselor to help you reverse the self-destructive habits.

Meanwhile, I have even simpler advice for when you're tempted to have an outburst of angry words or actions: *Stop!* You can, and you must.

22 PRAY

When life gets especially difficult or dangerous, our natural human instinct is to pray. Whether to an unknown god, an idol, the sun, or the God we've learned about from the Bible, some deep well of desperation drives us to ask for help.

Among troops sent to battle zones in World War II, there was a significant occurrence of conversions to the Jesus of Christianity. They weren't necessarily seeking a religious experience; they were simply responding to a deep urge to seek help from a God they somehow knew was there. Many of these "foxhole conversions" were lasting—these men returned home after the war having been changed forever by their prayers.

I pray every morning. It's part of my getting ready for the day. I pray for my children and grandchildren, for my friends, and about issues I'm confronting and decisions to be made. I'm much the better for it. I feel more connected and in tune with what's important.

By the way, I'm not talking about stilted religious prayers filled with flowery words and phrases one would never use in ordinary conversation. Forget that idea. I'm talking about a simple conversation with God in ordinary words you would use talking with a friend.

And it's private. No one's listening, except God.

I recently spoke about this with a friend who had very little by way of belief. I told her, "Just pray and say, 'God, if You're there, reveal Yourself to me.' Then go on and talk to God." There's something soothing about this kind of conversational approach to prayer.

Should you pray out loud? That's up to you. It may make you feel more connected, but God doesn't care whether you pray silently or actually speak.

I have friends who talk aloud to themselves on the handball court. "Come on, you idiot," they'll say. "Watch the ball!" I'm not sure this helps their play, but it does get the mind and mouth working together. Maybe it will be the same for you in prayer.

You might feel some resistance to this kind of prayer. You're thinking, *How can I talk casually and conversationally with God as though we're old friends, when that's not really the case? Isn't that being a hypocrite?* But don't we do something similar all the time? We speak warmly and conversationally with strangers we've just met, or with customers whose business we want, or in all kinds of situations. It's all just part of getting along.

To God, our very act of praying to Him is honoring because

it's an honest admission of our dependence on Him. The Bible says that God "will respond to the prayer of the destitute; he will not despise their plea."[4]

What should you pray for? The Bible says we're to pray about "everything" and to also include "thanksgiving."[5] Does that mean you'll get *everything* you ask for in prayer? No way. But along with this command to pray (instead of worry) about everything, the Bible goes on to hold out the promise of experiencing "the peace of God, which transcends all understanding."[6]

Even if you don't understand much about prayer's meaning or process, pray. Talk to God and see where it leads you. God does listen.

GIVE MONEY

Giving is one of the great joys of life. When our children are young, we give freely and joyfully and hardly think of it as sacrifice. We love to give to see the responses of their smiles and uninhibited pleasure. We also give when they have no idea they're receiving as we save for their college expenses, provide them with food and clothing, and so much more.

The principle of giving should extend far beyond our immediate family. Giving to one's church and to mission agencies is important, especially because God is the ultimate source of all our income and possessions: "It is he who gives you the ability to produce wealth."[7] It all belongs to Him, and we're stewards of what He has given us.

But our giving should extend even wider still. One of the most inwardly rewarding experiences is to give to those who can never repay the gift: the poor, the homeless, orphans, widows, and the downtrodden.

Look especially for deserving and needy young people to help. When I entered college, my parents were unable to help me financially. A businessman, my lifelong mentor, gave me five hundred dollars to help me get through my freshman year. Later, when I tried to repay him, he simply told me to give to someone else—which I did. He made a meaningful investment in me and taught me a great lesson of giving.

The easiest commodity to give is money. In America we have the unusual privilege of receiving a tax deduction for our charitable giving. But that deduction should never be the motive for giving—it simply allows us to give more.

Be generous and you'll never regret it. As wise Solomon said, "Give freely and become more wealthy; be stingy and lose everything. The generous will prosper; those who refresh others will themselves be refreshed."[8]

GIVE TIME

It's relatively easy to give money; the really costly donation is the gift of our time, the one diminishing resource of our lives. Time *is* life. So to give time is to give our lives.

A friend came up to me recently and said, "Can you give me ten minutes of your life?" I think he sensed my busyness, but he also identified the most significant thing I could give him then: my time.

To whom should we give our time? First, to our spouses, children, and other extended family; then to our friends and coworkers; and then to others.

A Hallmark card will never replace your presence. Funerals and baptisms, birthdays and bar mitzvahs, your children's soccer games and concerts—all deserve your presence. Special events such as award presentations and graduations top the list. Being there for all of these will demonstrate a spirit of giving.

In terms of service to others, writing a check is easy. But

serving at your local soup kitchen, working in a poor village to dig a well or construct a building, taking meals to people in grief or illness, visiting the ill and aged—these speak volumes of true compassion for others because they're costly giving.

GIVE YOURSELF

The famous psychologist Karl Menninger was asked how to treat depression and despondency. He said he would tell the person to get out of the house, go to a poor part of town, and help someone. "To overcome discouragement," he said, "don't focus on yourself; get involved in the lives of other people."

We spend most of our lives serving ourselves. We work to make money to buy both necessities and items of comfort. We sacrifice to get ahead in position, power, and prestige. We save to buy trinkets and toys to fill our leisure time. Yet we often feel empty and unfulfilled. For a while, the challenge of work and accomplishment keeps us motivated. Then it dulls in its attraction.

There must be something more.

That something more is often found in giving yourself to something bigger than your own desires—something that ties your heart and mind to a greater purpose, a greater good.

A few decades ago, a young man named Millard Fuller

was driven to succeed. By age twenty-nine, he had graduated from law school, started a business, and become a millionaire. However, it was destroying his marriage, his health, and, more important, his ethical standards.

In disillusionment, he began to search. His search led him to both a renewed commitment as a follower of Christ and reconciliation with his wife, Linda. Then both he and Linda took the drastic step of selling all their possessions and giving the money to the poor.

As they continued searching for how to make a deeper contribution with their lives, they discovered Koinonia Farm, a Christian community focused on applying Christ's teaching by helping people in practical ways. They were inspired by the farm's founders, Clarence and Florence Jordan, who were also involved in helping Americans during the civil rights movement.

After discovering from Clarence Jordan that housing was a critical issue for the poor, Millard Fuller decided to do something about it. Thus, Habitat for Humanity was born. The Fullers recruited low-income families to help build their own houses, also recruiting others to help and invest both time and money. At one point, the Fullers moved to Africa with their four children to do the same kind of work.

Today, Habitat for Humanity International is one of the most effective forces in helping the poor. It came about all because one man decided to give himself to a larger purpose and make a difference.

You might say, "Great story, but that's not me." It's true you might not do something as monumental as starting Habitat for Humanity, but you can do *something*. Get involved in something bigger than yourself and your material goals. Go help build a Habitat for Humanity house, or go on a mission trip with your church or some organization. Organize a car care clinic to help single moms. Get involved in the local version of the Special Olympics. Help an organization reaching out to street kids. Give time and support to teen assistance programs or to crisis pregnancy centers.

The list is endless. Just look around your community and you'll find plenty to do. And as you get involved and start helping others, you'll be astounded at how much it will do for you as well.

My friend Steve Bigari owned several McDonald's restaurants. He saw that his employees couldn't afford housing or transportation since they couldn't qualify for loans. He personally guaranteed some loans for them and has encouraged the local financial community to partner with him to help the working poor. He doesn't give them money but gives them opportunity and a way out. Steve recounted his story in his book *The Box You Got*. He went on to create the American Family Organization (amfol.com).

"Take what you have," Steve says, "and make a difference today. (1) Start right *where you are*: your life, your job, your family; (2) Start *today*; (3) Make a decision to be a change-maker, to make a difference in people's lives."

Another friend, Mary Jane Ponten, who was affected with cerebral palsy and nearing age eighty, began Mephibosheth Ministries to teach people how to relate to the handicapped and help them. She teaches in schools and travels to other countries. She's making a difference. There were times that Mary Jane wiped down tables at a local McDonald's to keep bread on the table, but she wouldn't quit making a difference and giving herself. (Her late husband, Bud, also had cerebral palsy. He was one of my respected mentors when I was a teenager and throughout my adult life.)

Get out of yourself and get into helping others. You'll never regret it, and you'll never be the same.

WATCH OUT FOR ICEBERGS

Icebergs — so beautiful, yet so dangerous — typically have about 90 percent of their volume below the water's surface where they float.

That's the way life is: filled with incredible beauty above and hidden danger below. We float about beholding the beauty, taking the risk of losing our flimsy shell of protection either by unseen danger or foolish risks.

What are some of these icebergs we face?

Moral temptations. Men look to the beauty of body and face, turning away from their marriage vows or their moral compass. The Bible (as well as other great wisdom literature) warns against this kind of moral failure:

The lips of a seductive woman are oh so sweet,
 her soft words are oh so smooth.
But it won't be long before she's gravel in your mouth,

a pain in your gut, a wound in your heart.
She's dancing down the primrose path to Death;
    she's headed straight for Hell and taking you with
        her. . . .

So, my friend, listen closely;
    don't treat my words casually.
Keep your distance from such a woman;
    absolutely stay out of her neighborhood.
You don't want to squander your wonderful life,
    to waste your precious life among the hardhearted.[9]

The same temptation trips up women (it takes two), though it's often not physical beauty that appeals to her but the beauty of being listened to, taken seriously, and understood. Yet "she hasn't a clue about Real Life, about who she is or where she's going."[10]

Moral icebergs impede us throughout life, always looking so attractive yet bringing disaster in their wake.

Craving wealth. Business books and media advertisements are constantly promoting an easy way to wealth and success. Having wealth isn't evil; wealth is good. But how one gets it, or what is sacrificed along the way, reveals the iceberg.

So often, wealth is pursued in devious ways. Even when it isn't, the sacrifices of other priorities often choke our future. If obtaining wealth means neglecting one's family, ethics, principles, or self-esteem, that's far too high a price to pay. Besides, "wealth" is only a relative term. It's so uncertain and so inadequate. No matter how much you have, you always desire more.

So be cautious on buying into that path. But if wealth comes your way and you can still avoid the adverse side roads, then enjoy it and be generous.

Busyness. Many of us run through life so busy and occupied that we simply don't have time to enjoy life. Our busyness undermines marriage, communication, and family life. We need to slow down our pace and intensity—for our health, our sanity, and the pleasures of soaking in the beauty of life and relationships. We need to cultivate what Gordon MacDonald calls our "spiritual garden":

> When this garden is in proper order, it is a quiet place, and there is an absence of busyness, of defiling noise. The inner garden is a delicate place, and if not properly maintained, it will be quickly overrun by intrusive undergrowth.[11]

One of the things that contribute most to excessive busyness is our saying yes to pursuits and responsibilities that are worthwhile in and of themselves but not necessarily the right thing for us at this particular time. Opportunities abound, but not every one has our name on it. Our marriage and family must come first. The iceberg is there when we run after glorious opportunities to the neglect of primary responsibilities.

WHAT *NOT* TO DO

No set of rules would be complete without a list of "don'ts." That's something we learn early on as children: *Don't run out in the street, don't get into a car with a stranger, don't let the dog drink from the toilet bowl*, and so on.

In this book, I take a mostly positive approach to rules, but there are some critical "don'ts" that can't be ignored:

- Don't be an egotist; you're not that hot!
- Don't give up when life is hard.
- Don't get into debt.
- Don't spend more than you make.
- Don't give up on your marriage; it's worth fighting for.
- Don't cheat on your spouse.
- Don't cheat on your employer.
- Don't neglect your children.
- Don't neglect your parents.

- Don't abandon your friends.
- Don't drink alcohol excessively; it will come back to bite you, physically and socially.
- Don't do drugs. Ever.
- Don't smoke.
- Don't use profanity; there are better ways to communicate.
- Don't put other people down or speak badly of them.
- Don't be dishonest in business, finances, or speech.
- Don't betray confidences.
- Don't give up on God and religion.

RELATIONSHIP
RULES

TREAT PEOPLE WELL

In our hostile workaday world, the people we meet desire and deserve three things from us:

1. *Honor*—for who they are, not for what they do.
2. *Respect*—regardless of their gifting, position, or status.
3. *Love*—which is the unconditional acceptance of their personhood.

We can impart these three things to others through our attitudes, words, body language, actions, and expenditure of time.

Everyone desires and equally deserves our honor, respect, and love because each human being is fashioned in the image of God. That's why we're to affirm the dignity and value of every person. There will always be those who are smarter, more gifted, wealthier, or more powerful, as well as those who are less endowed in all those ways. But there are no "lesser people."

Neurosurgeons, janitors, fast-food cooks, pilots, homemakers, theologians, migrant workers, actors, widows, presidents—all are human; all have feelings and needs.

In my Air Force career, I observed that it was the enlisted men and women and the younger officers who really did the work. In a factory, it's the assembly-line workers who actually produce things, though they don't receive the attention their supervisors do. But whether working on the line or as a supervisor, every person makes a contribution and should be treated with dignity.

In our culture today, the very young as well as the elderly are often marginalized and disrespected. As Mary and I have grown older, we've observed that younger people often ignore us—until they discover "who" we are and find out more about our backgrounds, and then their attitude changes. Thankfully that's not true everywhere in this world; in many cultures, age is still respected, at least outwardly.

The Golden Rule is always true: "Do to others as you would have them do to you."[12] You know what it's like when people look down on you, snub you, insult you. You feel devalued, embarrassed, angry, or ashamed. It's devastating. Never give others reason to feel that way because of how you treat them.

Jesus was a great role model in this. He constantly paid attention to the rejected, the outcasts, the unclean. He dined with people with sinful reputations and extended help to those who were socially or physically deprived.

Jesus also spoke this categorical command: "Love your neighbor as yourself."[13] Another passage in the Bible expresses it this way: "Get along with each other; don't be stuck-up. Make friends with nobodies; don't be the great somebody."[14]

29 COMPLIMENT PEOPLE

"Hey, you played a great game. I love that last shot you made." Your son hears it all—and remembers—even if his team lost in a rout. Your words are more powerful than the score.

During my senior year in high school, I took American History under Mr. Livingston, a demanding teacher. He'd given me a C when I was a freshman, but I was determined to do better this time around. One day I gave an oral report in his class on a Civil War battle. When I sat down, he said, "Now, that's the way a report should be given." So few words, but so remembered—so encouraging to a young man from the wrong side of the tracks. I kept in touch with Mr. Livingston all his life, until he died at age 104.

Why criticize when you can compliment? Why point out faults when you can commend a person? What works with children works equally well with adults. We all need to be affirmed.

I'm doing this much better with my grandchildren than I

did with my own children. Why didn't I do it as well with my children? My youth and inexperience as a parent were certainly factors. Having parental authority over my children made my words doubly powerful. Your work as a boss, parent, or spouse carries influence you hardly knew you had.

It's easy to compliment, so look for ways to do it often. Compliment the way a person dresses, or completes a task at work or at home, or offers a sacrificial service, or achieves a personal goal. Look for the good things a person is or does.

Here are a few guidelines for giving compliments:

- Be sincere. Don't use empty flattery.
- Be truthful.
- Don't make a big deal out of it; just do it.
- Be an equal complimenter. Don't play favorites.

Ken Blanchard and Spencer Johnson, in their book *The One-Minute Manager*, started a revolution with this single suggestion: "Catch someone doing something good, and tell them."

I remember well the sparkle in my children's and grandchildren's eyes when I commended them. I also remember the loyalty that ensued when I did the same for people who worked for me. I especially remember how it changed the atmosphere with my dear wife, Mary, when I spoke well of her incredible mothering.

Compliment people. Doing so is one of the most valuable gifts you can give.

30   Be Real

Most of us go through life trying to please other people: parents, peers, bosses, the opposite sex. As a result, many of us spend a lot of time pretending to be something other than what we really are.

When we live like this, we develop an emotional schizophrenia or a chameleon-like personality. We delude ourselves into thinking no one sees past our masquerade. The reality is that almost everyone recognizes the truth about us.

So you may as well be real—be yourself.

Of course, we always have a number of different roles and relationships, and we talk and act differently in many of these roles. How we interact with a boss or client just isn't the same as how we respond to a friend or coworker, and that, in turn, looks much different from how we relate to our children. But in all of our relationships, there must be an inner sameness that allows our true character to color our role. The outward expression will change, but the inward attitude is consistent.

God gave you a unique personality with its unique attractiveness as well as its rough spots. As you mature, you begin to develop and modify your expression of this personality. Unfortunately, in some ways, you learn to hide who you really are.

How can you be more authentic and still function in appropriate ways in each of your roles and relationships?

- Know and understand yourself. Self-discovery isn't always easy; we're easily deceived by our prejudices about ourselves. Taking a temperament analysis test or a similar evaluation can be helpful.
- Be self-aware. Know when your manner of speaking and acting differs significantly from one situation to the next. Begin a process of constantly adjusting to be more consistent.
- Be truly focused on other people. Listen to them. Be genuinely caring and concerned. This will help you guard against a professional façade.
- Get feedback from friends and family. They see you for who you really are.

My basic counsel here is this: *Don't be a phony.*

31

BE AVAILABLE

Ever found yourself responding in ways like these:

- "Sorry, son, I'm just too busy. I'll catch your next game."
- "Mom, I know it's your birthday, but we're just overbooked."
- "I know, dear, it would be great to take that vacation. We just can't fit it in this summer."

I'm still plagued by the memory of times when I wasn't available. I once discovered that a friend had been going through some deep waters in his life. I asked why he hadn't called me. His answer was something I've heard all too often: "Well, I know you're so busy."

Too many times I haven't been available for people and the important events in their lives, so I've had to change both the way I live and what people—especially my family and close friends—see in my life.

It's important to be available. That doesn't mean you can't be busy, even very busy. It *does* mean you need availability to the important people in your life, and sometimes even to people you haven't met before.

Availability is particularly true in developing and maintaining friendships. "I've often been in the company of those who complain that they have no friends," said the French writer Ignace Lepp. "Inevitably, I've observed that this condition was due to their own lack of availability; they were too encumbered to be able to welcome another."

Availability is also needed in the spiritual realm of our lives. Neal A. Maxwell stated it this way: "God does not begin by asking us about our ability, but only about our availability; and if we then prove our dependability, he will increase our capability."

Although it's contrary to standard time-management advice, I keep my office door open most of the time. It's a symbol of availability. Obviously, you can't be available to everyone at all times—not even your family—but it's important to convey the spirit, impression, and communication of availability. Work to cultivate an unhurried and open demeanor even in the midst of a busy life.

32 DISAGREE AGREEABLY

One of life's constants is that you'll never be in total agreement about everything with anyone—your spouse, your children, your coworkers, your neighbors, or your friends. That isn't bad in itself. But how we conduct ourselves in disagreeing can be a real negative. Disagreeing agreeably is a skill that can and should be developed.

The first key question to ask yourself is this: "*When* should I express my disagreement?" In many situations, the issue isn't really important enough to call anything into question. But if it is worth discussing, the next key question is this: "*How* should I express my disagreement?"

Often we can easily detect when someone disagrees with us. A raised eyebrow, a certain change in tone of voice, or a questioning look will reveal it almost immediately. If you sense that, encourage them to speak up and express their thoughts. Don't make them feel they're rejecting you if they reject your ideas.

Meanwhile, if you're the one with the raised eyebrow or the questioning look as you're listening to someone else, learn to respond calmly with words such as these:

- "Help me understand a little more of your thinking."
- "You may well be right. I need to think about it a bit more."
- "I've thought about that too. Here are some ideas I've wondered about . . ."

Instead it's all too easy for words and actions to communicate an attitude that tells others, "Your idea is really stupid. Let me straighten you out."

When there's disagreement, here are some good approaches I've found that work well:

- Be sure you understand what the other person said. Ask clarifying questions.
- Use equivocal and affirming expressions:

  - "I appreciate knowing how you think."
  - "That's a good observation. I'd like to weigh it more carefully."
  - "I see you've given that a lot of thought. Have you considered . . . ?"
  - "I come at that from a different perspective, but you stated your view well."

- Never attack the person. Let him know that your acceptance of him isn't altered just because you have differing viewpoints.
- Even in a direct confrontation about more serious matters, you can affirm the person and value the relationship. "Respectfully, I need to differ on that. Could we look at it like this . . . ?"
- Be cautious in disagreeing with someone in the presence of others. Try to express your disagreement in private so as not to embarrass the other person.

Sometimes during a discussion in which I disagree with what's being said, I've chosen not to engage simply because I didn't think it would have been particularly helpful. In those situations, there's always the danger of being perceived as wishy-washy or indifferent, which is better than coming across as obnoxious or arrogant.

I've operated in many work situations where disagreement and arguments are almost a daily occurrence. I've found that seasoned relationships and the kind of mutual respect that has developed over time will lay the foundation for healthy disagreement and debate. One of the keys is to admit you're not always right; another is to be willing to compromise. If you have a reputation of being someone who refuses to change his or her mind, it can kill healthy dialogue. If others see you that way—especially in your family—then some significant changes are needed, and perhaps even an apology.

Whenever you sense you've gone too far in disagreeing, go to the person and ask if you caused any offense, and if so, make it right.

33 SPEAK GENTLY AND BE KIND

Harsh and unkind words destroy relationships. Whether with your spouse, children, coworkers, or friends, such words poison relationships for years to come.

In my military career, I've known of a number of generals who had reputations for gruffness and a confrontational style of leadership. Some would yell at people who briefed them, and some would storm out of meetings when they felt the presenter hadn't done his homework. Another always checked to see if his subordinates were wearing the required over-the-calf socks.

I sat in one time when two young officers were briefing a general. I was there as a colonel in a consultant role. The general munched on his lunch while the two young officers talked. Then he tore into them, berating them in front of me.

These generals were feared, grudgingly accepted, and promoted if they got results. But they were seldom respected.

Here's a better picture: One of my friends had to brief a

general when he was a young lieutenant. He arrived at work and realized he'd forgotten his necktie for his dress uniform. Not having time to go home and get it, he decided to wear his raincoat buttoned to the top. It aroused intrigue. The general asked, "Son, is it raining in here?"

"No, sir."

"Well, what's with the raincoat?"

"Sir, I forgot my uniform tie."

"Lieutenant, take off your coat. Okay, everyone, remove your neckties. Let's get on with the briefing."

What a difference!

To put it bluntly, there's *never* a reason for harshness and unkindness. You can speak strongly and powerfully in correction and discipline without abusive language.

Solomon got it right:

A gentle response defuses anger,
    but a sharp tongue kindles a temper-fire. . . .
Kind words heal and help;
    cutting words wound and maim.[15]

Learn to speak gently and be kind.

In my world of work in the Air Force and in other leadership roles, I found that my words and manner of speaking carried much more weight than I realized. After one reprimand to a colonel, he wrote a note back to me with the single phrase "Mea culpa" — *my fault.* My message got across to him, but I'd probably gone beyond kind words.

My children still have recollections of my speaking harshly to them. They may not remember them all, thankfully, but still the memories form the basis of parent-child relationships for a lifetime. I wish I could take back those harsh words and rephrase them.

For those of us who tend to have a cynical twist of mind, the task of speaking gently is more difficult. Whatever the topic, we like to cut, chop, and criticize. Especially when someone is bringing forth an argument with which we don't quite agree, we can too easily resort to cynical, cutting words rather than a reasoned discussion.

This poem, by an unknown author, illustrates well some of these thoughts:

> I ran into a stranger as he passed by.
> "Oh, excuse me please" was my reply.
>
> He said, "Please excuse me too;
> I wasn't watching for you."
>
> We were very polite, this stranger and I.
> We went on our way, and we said good-bye.
>
> But at home a different story is told,
> how we treat our loved ones, young and old.

Later that day, cooking the evening meal,
My son stood beside me very still.

When I turned, I nearly knocked him down.
"Move out of the way," I said with a frown.

He walked away, his little heart broken.
I didn't realize how harshly I'd spoken.

While I lay awake in bed,
God's still small voice came to me and said,

"While dealing with a stranger, common courtesy you use,
But the children you love, you seem to abuse.

"Go and look on the kitchen floor,
You'll find some flowers there by the door.

"Those are the flowers he brought for you.
He picked them himself: pink, yellow, and blue.

"He stood very quietly not to spoil the surprise,
And you never saw the tears that filled his little eyes."

By this time, I felt very small,
And now my tears began to fall.

I quietly went and knelt by his bed;
"Wake up, little one, wake up," I said.

"Are these the flowers you picked for me?"
He smiled, "I found them, out by the tree.

"I picked them because they're pretty, like you.
I knew you'd like them, especially the blue."

I said, "Son, I'm very sorry for how I acted today;
I shouldn't have yelled at you that way."

He said, "Oh, Mom, that's okay.
I love you anyway."

I said, "Son, I love you too,
and I do like the flowers, especially the blue."

Speak kindly, speak gently — then you will never have to eat
your words.

SAY "THANK YOU"

Appreciation and affirmation motivate people more than money and rewards. Not that money and appropriate rewards are insignificant, but people want to be valued and appreciated for what they do and who they are.

A sincerely worded "thank you," accompanied by eye contact, conveys a powerful message; a brusque or perfunctorily mumbled "thanks" won't do it.

Expressing gratitude to our young children is a way to reinforce obedience and good actions: "Jordan, thank you for picking up your toys. That was a very helpful thing to do." We've all built pride and resolve into our children in this way, which is far superior to scolding and threats.

Why do we forget or neglect to do the same with adults? Possibly because we're in a hurry. Or we're thinking, *That's his job. No thanks is needed.* But we each long for affirmation when we do our jobs well. The waitress, the janitor, the boss, the service station attendant, the teacher of our children, the clerk in the hardware store—all need thanks and affirmation. Take the time and make a point of paying attention to them.

And when possible, add specifics: "Thanks so much for helping me find the right size." "Thank you for checking back to see if we needed anything." "Thank you for teaching my son; he really likes your class." "Thank you for the way you just helped that elderly gentleman when he couldn't find the right change." "Thank you for working on this holiday; I'm sure you would like to be at home."

So much of life is functional and perfunctory. A word of appreciation simply puts flesh and feeling to our connections with people.

So many work and serve while receiving little or no thanks. Let's make their day better.

And don't forget to do this especially with your family. They need it too.

CALL BACK

How many times have you left a voice mail, sent an e-mail, or left a callback request with a business or doctor's office or secretary and heard nothing? Often. Too many times. What kind of thoughts does that make you have about the person or business you called? *Negative* is a soft description.

- *They don't care enough to call back.*
- *They don't really want my business.*
- *They don't want to talk to me.*

Frustration sets in as you e-mail again ("Just wondered if you got my first e-mail") or call again and press the number options until you finally speak to a real person (or give up trying).

Now put the shoes on your feet and remember how often you haven't returned a call or answered an e-mail request. (I'm not talking about sales calls or spam e-mails but contacts from people you know.) Why didn't you respond?

- You had the best of intentions but forgot.
- You planned to reply later but just haven't yet.
- You really didn't want to respond.

Obviously, you can't shove all other priorities aside in order to respond immediately to every call or e-mail you get from a friend or acquaintance. But at least acknowledge the call or message. Just call back or send a quick e-mail: "Got your note. I'll respond next week." People deserve that connection. Customers value that commitment.

Is there a hierarchy of who to respond to and when? Of course. My children take first priority. My grandchildren can't wait until tomorrow: "Bapa, I need your help on my science project. And it's due tomorrow!" Close friends should always get through. Treat them the way you like to be treated.

Recently I was at a conference where several four-star generals in the Air Force were speaking. After one speech, I talked to one general about an issue. I gave him my card. He said he would have someone check on it. To my surprise, a few days later I received a call from one of his top deputies. That impressed me.

The Bible adds an interesting perspective on this: "He who is faithful in a very little thing is faithful also in much."[16] A "very little thing" like getting back with people promptly may cost you some time, but it says a lot about what kind of person you really are.

DON'T CARRY A GRUDGE

Holding a grudge and seeking revenge is like preparing a poison drink for your enemy and drinking it yourself. It ultimately destroys you, not the other person.

Throughout your life, other people will hurt you, cheat you, offend you, or betray you in an attempt to undermine your success or reputation. Welcome to the real world. In those situations, your initial responses—anger, hurt, sadness, panic—can rarely be stifled. But those are short-term and immediate responses. In the long term, you might sometimes begin to nurture grudges and plot revenge—or at least hope for some payback to the ones who hurt you. This is disastrous. Why is it so harmful?

First, the person who's hurt the most is you. Your grudging feelings will be constant, coloring almost everything you do. They'll adversely affect you at both work and home. They'll rob your mind of rationality and creative thinking. They'll sap your energy and emotions. These results often are not immediately apparent except when the initial offense is so raw and real. But over time, your inner being will be quietly eaten away.

Second, the desire for revenge robs you of personal joy and satisfaction. It focuses too much of your energy on seeking to repay the wrong.

What should you do to keep from grudges and revenge?

- Put it behind you. You can't rewind time and undo what's happened, so let it go.
- Forgive the person who caused the problem. Forgiveness is actually the first step to healing yourself. It will free your mind, unlock your emotions, and allow you to move to the future. "Forgiveness is almost a selfish act," writes Lawana Blackwell, "because of its immense benefits to the one who forgives."
- Make the commitment not to damage your relationships, especially in your family, by actions that increase conflict or tension.
- Where possible, keep communication alive and allow healing to occur. When tension and hurt are present, often it's due primarily to misunderstandings and unintended offenses rather than to anyone's purposeful actions.

The Bible's counsel on this is wise: "As far as it depends on you, live at peace with everyone."[17]

MAKE AND KEEP CLOSE FRIENDS

Even though Mary and I have written a book on building friendships, I still find myself longing for more friendships and puzzling over the strange bond that makes a friendship deep and meaningful.

Many of us would say that we have many friends, when the reality is that most are simply acquaintances or work associates or neighbors. They're not the ones we would call in a crisis.

Throughout our lives, particularly when we were young, we may have had one or two "best friends." Where did those friendships go? Time, events, and geography separate us. I was talking with a businessman who'd often had to relocate because of his work, and he was telling me about the pain this caused from being so frequently uprooted from friendships. "But I've solved the problem," he said. "Now I just don't make any friends." That's sad.

We have many *acquaintances*—hundreds of them. We make

them almost daily in the course of life. We also have *casual friends*: people whose names we remember and who are in our circles of life and work. Most people can easily sustain fifty to a hundred relationships at this level. We greet these people when we see them, but rarely do we socialize.

On a higher level are *close friends*: people we see frequently and socialize with. This is the level of friendship we most commonly think of when we hear the word *friends*. You probably sustain from a dozen to as many as thirty of these friendships at any given time in your life.

Close friendships are more than a pleasure — they're vital to our health. In *Ten Essentials of Highly Healthy People*, Dr. Walt Larimore connects poor health factors such as high cholesterol levels, heart disease, and high blood pressure to lack of relationships. "Reducing loneliness by developing and enhancing friendships will improve your overall health," he writes. "You don't need a large group of friends; a small group will do. Even one or two close friends with whom you share interests and affection can do the trick."

It's well worth the effort it takes to maintain and keep close friendships. What are the primary barriers to forming such friendships? I think of five:

Time. Every relationship takes time: time to talk, time to meet, time to e-mail, time to socialize. We need to be willing to invest the time it takes to allow friendships to develop and deepen. This can be costly.

Lack of common interests. Every friendship needs mutual interests: children, school, sports, community activities, church, clubs, political or social causes. Friendships don't happen just because we're neighbors or coworkers. Seek out people who share your interests and passions.

Disparity among couples. Men may develop friendships with other men and women with other women but may not be friends as couples. If you're married, couple-to-couple friendships give great pleasure but are slower to develop and take more effort. And because women normally drive the level of social interaction, couple-to-couple friendships will be easier to develop if the wives are already close friends.

Distance. Many friendships wane when geography makes contact difficult. The mobility of our work world intervenes and interrupts our friendships. We must be more deliberate in our efforts to stay connected to keep the friendships alive.

Conflict. I've never seen an enduring friendship that didn't suffer from some level of conflict along the way. Conflict comes from many sources: children not getting along, harsh words, misunderstanding or miscommunication, an argument, changing values, and more. A long-term friendship must survive conflict and some level of disagreement. We need to be able to reconcile and overlook our differences. Unfortunately, some conflicts never get resolved and break the friendship. That is real life.

What will build and develop close friendships? The strongest igniter of close friendships is your decision to seek and develop them. Here are other factors:

- Mutual attraction
- Mutual interests
- Social time together
- Shared activities
- A shared commitment to stay connected

Make and Keep Intimate Friends

For a meaningful life, we desperately need not only close friends but also what I call *intimate friends*: the people with whom we have the deepest, lifelong relationships.

These friends are much more than golf buddies or card-game partners; they're the people you could call in the middle of the night when you face a crisis. We'll probably never have more than three to five of these intimate friendships at any single point in our lives.

Solomon said, "There is a friend who sticks closer than a brother."[18] We need friends who stick with us through the hard times—who we care for deeply and who care for us. Friends like that don't just happen. In fact, they're rare. They must be purposefully developed and nurtured.

We're fortunate to have such friends. After our son was killed, three couples—our intimate friends—dropped everything they were doing and flew to our aid from various parts of the country. They didn't need to be asked; they just did it. We cannot put a price on such friendships.

Be intentional about making friends who are there for a lifetime.

MEET WITH A SMALL GROUP

The last thing many people want is more meetings! We're already too busy, too pressed and stressed, to add anything to our schedules.

We sometimes work on teams in our job, or serve on committees, or go to church. As good and necessary as these activities are, most people fail to have the kind of small-group encounters with other people that are most fulfilling and needed.

I've found that I need to be part of a small group of friends who meet regularly around a common goal or interest. These are people who aren't required to come together but *choose* to.

In such a group, there's an openness of sharing and discussion on life issues everyone is facing. Marriage, children, work, personal struggles, and career issues are open for discussion.

Such a group can be focused around many interests, such as these:

- Raising children
- Book discussions
- Bible discussions
- Developing friendships
- Special business interests
- Marriage development
- Cooking
- Spirituality

Mary and I have found that certain characteristics are common and necessary to make such a group work well:

- Meet regularly (twice a month is a reasonable goal).
- Keep it small (eight to ten people seems ideal).
- Have commonality in your age, stage of life, and interests.
- Have a leader or facilitator.
- Articulate a purpose and a focus, and stick to it. Be flexible but also persistent.
- Adjust to people's needs rather than being confined to an agenda.
- Try it for at least a few months, then rethink and reevaluate before deciding to continue.

Mary and I have met with several groups over the years, and this has been one of the most rewarding and encouraging activities of our lives. What do we get out of it?

- Deep friendships, many for a lifetime
- Stimulation and reflection
- Accountability
- Help and support in times of suffering, trouble, and stress
- Fun

Such groups don't just happen. They need to be thoughtfully created and developed.

40 Make Love

Got your attention, didn't I?

But sex isn't love. Even the term "making love" is almost a perversion of the true concept of love.

Love is such a big idea. We make a life by loving people. When we make love a primary focus of our lives, we enrich everyone around us. All the accomplishments and successes of life will not be remembered at your funeral, but your attitude and actions of love will be.

People who truly love others leave an incredibly valuable legacy. As I write this, it's graduation week in our city. Again and again I see the students honor teachers who loved them. I've never heard them mention what a phenomenal teacher of algebra or geography they were. The students respond to these teachers because they showed the students love in how they cared for them.

Learn to love. Decide to make love permeate your life and

relationships. Love your family, of course, but also love your employers, your coworkers, your boss, and your neighbors.

Take to heart the most eloquent statement about love ever written:

Love never gives up.
Love cares more for others than for self.
Love doesn't want what it doesn't have.
Love doesn't strut,
Doesn't have a swelled head,
Doesn't force itself on others,
Isn't always "me first,"
Doesn't fly off the handle,
Doesn't keep score of the sins of others,
Doesn't revel when others grovel,
Takes pleasure in the flowering of truth,
Puts up with anything,
Trusts God always,
Always looks for the best,
Never looks back,
But keeps going to the end.

Love never dies.[19]

ENHANCING
YOUR WORK AND
EFFECTIVENESS

WORK HARD

A farmer knows what hard work is. I remember the summers on my grandparents' farm in Iowa. Everyone worked hard. Grandma White labored all day—in the kitchen, in the garden, feeding the chickens, and doing so many other tasks. From early morning until late afternoon, work consumed everyone. There was little choice if the farm were to succeed and survive.

When most of the world had an agrarian-based economy, all the family, even young children, worked. Only a few in the ruling classes had any concept of a life of laziness and leisure, or any opportunity for it. Later, in the industrial age, factory work became drudgery, with supervisors forcing people to work hard for long hours.

In today's knowledge-based society and work world, leisure and laziness have become possible for many. But who prospers and gets ahead? The one who works hard. Whether you're a student, a laborer, or a manager, hard work pays off.

Solomon understood that. "All hard work brings a profit," he wrote, "but mere talk leads only to poverty."[20]

And listen to his advice to the "lazy fool":

Look at an ant.
     Watch it closely; let it teach you a thing or two.
Nobody has to tell it what to do.
     All summer it stores up food;
     at harvest it stockpiles provisions.
So how long are you going to laze around doing nothing?
     How long before you get out of bed?
A nap here, a nap there, a day off here, a day off there,
     sit back, take it easy—do you know what comes next?
Just this: You can look forward to a dirt-poor life,
     poverty your permanent houseguest![21]

Why should you work hard?

- Doing so will reward you in the long run.
- You'll experience a deeper personal satisfaction.
- You'll set an example for your children.
- Your reputation will be enhanced.
- You'll develop lifelong good habits.

"Far and away the best prize that life offers," Theodore Roosevelt said, "is the chance to work hard at work worth doing."

The Scottish poet and writer Sir Theodore Martin called work "the true elixir of life" and added, "The busiest man is the happiest man."

But a word of caution: I'm not advocating being a workaholic. That's destructive to all concerned. Work hard and work *smart*. Don't sell your soul to your career and thereby neglect yourself and your family.

Here's what I mean by working hard:

- Give a full day's work for a full day's pay.
- Do more than just enough to get by.
- Don't give up when the task is difficult.
- Don't always quit when the clock says it's the end of the workday.
- Help others in their work.
- Keep learning how to do your work better.

I haven't always been the best at this. While working at Boeing Aircraft Company as a college student, I was reprimanded for talking to the other draftsmen too much. It really caught me up short. Never again was I going to be lax like that.

Watching people work is quite instructive. Some will lean on their shovels while others dig. Some lean on their elbows while others write. Some pretend to be busy, all the while impatiently waiting for the day to be over. Each of those who lean or look busy are the first to lose their jobs. But more than that, they lose their self-esteem.

"Hard work spotlights the character of people," Sam Ewing said. "Some turn up their sleeves, some turn up their noses, and some don't turn up at all." Hard work reveals your character, your commitment to excellence, and your respect for employers and your family.

I learned at an early age that I needed to work hard. I'm not naturally a hard worker at manual tasks, but that's what I cut my teeth on: working on a farm with my grandfather, sweeping floors and cleaning toilets at a seed company, and working on a construction crew. More than once I've had extremely boring jobs, but I found I still needed to work hard and do my best. It *always* paid off. Everyone notices a hard worker.

Yet I do remember my stepfather telling my mentor and employer that he was worried about my future because I had no skills. My mentor replied, "Don't worry about Jerry. He'll make his living with his mouth!" But he still drove me hard as I worked for him. He was a tough taskmaster. I learned much by working with him.

My stepfather was another great example. He always worked hard. Even in his sixties he was working on a freight company's loading dock, where he had to keep up with guys in their twenties while lifting and moving freight. He never complained. He just did what he had to do and did it well. Later he would relax from his arduous work by tending his flowers. He kept his garden as immaculate as the small house where we lived.

Mario Cuomo, former mayor of New York City, said he learned about working hard from his father. "I watched a small man with thick calluses on both hands work fifteen and sixteen hours a day . . . a man who came here uneducated, alone, unable to speak the language, who taught me all I needed to know about faith and hard work by the simple eloquence of his example."

42 Do Some Things Poorly

This advice seems to run counter to everything we've been taught since childhood. It's hard advice to follow, especially for perfectionists. The instruction to do what we're told to do—and do it well—still rings in our ears.

But there's not enough time in life for that. It's impossible to accomplish everything we're expected to do, or should do, or even want to do, if we think we have to do it all perfectly. Your capacity will be greatly diminished if you cannot discern what level of perfection is actually required in whatever you're doing.

In one of my first jobs as a teenager, I almost got fired for doing the job too well. I worked as a janitor at a seed company, sweeping floors and cleaning bathrooms. Occasionally they let me do more important things, such as filling sacks with five pounds of seed, using old balance scales to measure the right amount of seed. I was intent on making sure each sack balanced the scales perfectly, which meant I spent a lot of time with each sack full, going back and forth adding and taking away seed in the quest for the perfect measurement.

My boss was angry. He wanted me to quickly fill each sack until the scales balanced, then promptly top it off with just enough more seed to ensure the weight was over five pounds. He wanted production, not perfection!

Life is a series of daily, hard choices. The demands upon us are relentless, from life's simple tasks (eating, sleeping, exercising, talking to family, going to work) to the complex (growing a career, disciplining a child, buying a house, developing a skill, deciding to get married or divorced, serving on boards and committees). Life so easily becomes chaos when we try to do it all perfectly. The usual result is that some things fall by the wayside from neglect, especially those that are far down our intuitive priority list. We then become victim to our random choices or the inevitable demands of people around us.

That's no way to live.

We have to make choices. And the hardest choices are often about what *not* to do at all, or what to leave undone for the time being. These aren't always decisions we can make by ourselves; our families and employers might also play a part in our decisions, as they should. We might choose against their wishes, but we must live with the consequences.

We must also make hard choices with requests or invitations from others that would require our time commitment if we accept. Choosing to say no to the lesser gives us freedom to say yes to the best things.

So how do you decide (a) what must be done almost perfectly, (b) what's to be done at least fairly well, and (c) what's okay to be done only reasonably well? The deciding factors are the task at hand, your time, your ability, and your emotional well-being.

The task. Many chores, efforts, and responsibilities simply don't require the same level of performance that others do or carry the same weight of significance. Maintaining and repairing an airplane is a matter of life and death. Do it perfectly. Painting the back porch isn't crucial to anyone's safety or survival. Don't worry if it's not perfect.

Mary likes a clean house, and Mary's a perfectionist. But she once learned a valuable perspective when her aunt was talking about cleaning the house before guests arrive: "If they come looking for dust," she said, "I don't want to disappoint them!"

When you set out to work on a project, decide what level of completeness or perfection is needed or demanded.

Your time. Deadlines are wonderful things. A deadline forces you first to plan ahead and then finally to bring your effort to an end, whether or not you're fully done. Procrastination is deadly with deadlines. If an especially thorough job is required, starting late will always put you in an all-night panic. So try to start projects early and pace yourself toward completion.

Your ability. After receiving a word of correction from me, my children sometimes responded, "Well, no one's perfect!"

Very true, as my own example has proven to them many times. And our degree of imperfection varies greatly according to the task at hand. No matter how hard I try, I simply cannot do some tasks well. They're not in my skill set. Therefore, if I'm to do them, I must realize my limitations and either get help or live with the less-than-perfect results.

Your emotional well-being. Some of us waste an incredible amount of emotional energy trying to do everything perfectly. Some people are natural neatniks, and others are naturally messy. I'm the latter. For me, the cost of perfect neatness is horrendous. For the naturally neat person, it's much easier. But perfection isn't just a matter of tidiness. Even the natural drive to be perfect can affect many other areas and be an obsession that ultimately limits you.

Knowing yourself and tempering your self-expectation will guard you from emotional strain. For those of us who aren't perfectionists, we need to be a bit more diligent and conscientious. Those who are perfectionists need to loosen up. Both personality types need to counter natural tendencies in order to be well-rounded.

43 LEAVE SOME THINGS UNDONE

You've heard these words and maybe said them yourself: "Don't just sit there, do something!" I'd like to propose another statement to toss around now and then: "Just sit there, do nothing!"

One of the hard lessons to learn in life is that not everything that *can* be done *should* be done. In particular, not everything you *can* do should you do.

I'm not promoting procrastination or neglect. I'm talking about deliberate choices not to get immersed in busyness that just consumes your time with little result. Don't read every magazine or piece of junk mail; just throw it out. Don't answer every argument that comes your way. Don't respond to every need.

I recall being in a church where I was asked to lead the choir. I told them I couldn't. "But you're the only one who can do it," I was told. "Then God must not want us to have a choir," I responded with a bit of youthful arrogance.

You can choose not to grow flowers or plant a garden. You may choose not to install and use all that extra software on your computer. You can choose not to organize every paper on your desk.

Leaving things undone, however, must not simply increase another's workload unjustly. There are things that really must be done; if they're your responsibility, do them. Our family uses the word *schlutif* (passed down from Norwegian slang) for someone who's lazy and irresponsible. Don't be one of those people.

But also don't try to tackle everything that comes your way. Make good choices. Learn to filter opportunities. Otherwise, you'll be buried in a pile of unnecessary tasks.

44

Focus on Contribution, not Position

It's interesting to observe how people handle their positions of leadership and responsibility in a group, company, or organization. For some, their egos start to swell. Before long their identities get wrapped up in their positions. They get possessive about "their" power and "their" people and "their" promotions.

Perhaps that's because they attained their position of prominence only through their maneuvering and grasping for advantage. Of course, there's nothing dishonorable about being promoted to a position, and there's nothing wrong with ambition and achievement unless our motivation is for self-acclaim.

Other people in high positions exercise their responsibilities humbly, fulfilling their duties and making their contributions on behalf of others. They constantly ask, "What can I contribute?" instead of, "What can I gain?" When someone is motivated by contribution, he sees his position as a place of service, not a perk.

I once heard a four-star general discussing his responsibilities, using such phrases as "my people" and "my command." It was all about him. His ego was repulsive.

Another four-star general was asked how it felt to retire. He replied, "One moment I commanded thousands of soldiers, had incredible power and influence. The next moment my only command was the steering wheel of my car, and my wife told me where to turn it!" Not surprisingly, he died within two years.

Then there was Lieutenant General William K. Harrison, known as "the Christian general." He never received the field command he longed for. But he was chosen to be the first peace negotiator after the Korean War. When Harrison retired, he didn't have a moment's regret. He taught Scripture, wrote a book on eschatology, and helped many people grow spiritually. I remember his sitting in our home interacting with young Air Force cadets, passionately giving himself to what mattered deeply. What an inspiration!

Jesus once told His followers, "Whoever wants to become great among you must be your servant, and whoever wants to be first must be your slave."[22]

As leaders, we reap what we sow. Sowing to position reaps emptiness, but sowing to contribution reaps personal fulfillment. Let's be people who focus on meaningful contribution rather than mere position. If we do, we'll never be retired, unwanted, or unemployed.

45 LEARN TO WRITE WELL AND SPEAK WELL

Rightly or wrongly, people judge you by your communication. Especially in the world of business, the ability to write and speak well always makes you valuable.

Writing is a learned skill. Supposedly we learn to write in school, but that's often a weak area of education. As an engineer by training, I've had to develop writing skills largely on my own. Whether it's writing a business letter, a project report, a paragraph on one's personal goals for a job application, or making a request of one's employer, being able to use proper grammar and appropriate vocabulary will greatly increase its effectiveness.

How can you improve your writing? Consider taking a course at a junior college in writing, grammar, or speech (even if you have a PhD!). Keep a brief journal and write something every day.

Similar dynamics hold for how you speak. Consider joining

a Toastmasters club. Or teach a Sunday school class to children. They'll make you think and communicate!

You'll be amazed at the opportunities that open up as you improve yourself in writing and speaking.

46 MAKE LISTS

I'm an inveterate list maker. It may even be an obsession. But I think all of us create lists—in our minds at least, if not on paper. We have our grocery and shopping lists, our to-do lists at home and work, and our "get to it someday" lists. I've had lists of people to talk to, people to call, and ideas to further develop. I've had prioritized lists, daily lists, and more.

Why do lists help?

- They help you organize your day or week.
- They offload your memory and free your mind.
- They help keep you from forgetting things you need to do.
- They help you hold on to information that otherwise might be irretrievably lost.
- They relieve anxiety.

Mostly, lists help keep you organized, at least moderately. Everyone should develop his or her own system, but here's a simple approach:

Record your list on a sheet of paper, a 3x5 card, or whatever works best for you. Start with these helpful categories:

- *Do today*
- *Do later*
- *Contact* (by phone call or e-mail)
- *Remember* (items such as names, addresses, phone numbers, and so on, that can later be transferred elsewhere)

I often make a separate list for things to talk about with Mary, or with someone at work, or with some of the children.

Sometimes I number my list in order of priority, but often I just circle or highlight the most important items. When I've crossed off most of those, I simply copy onto another piece of paper what's undone and then toss the old list.

Do what works for you. And don't let people kid you about being a list maker.

47

COMPETE, BUT DON'T BE COMPETITIVE

Yes, it is possible to compete—and to compete well—without being driven by competitiveness.

The best examples come from sports. I play a lot of handball. I work at getting better, developing my shots, and increasing my skills. In the court, I play hard to win. But I'm not angry or derisive with my opponent. We'll be friends no matter who wins.

It's also true vocationally. In my Air Force career, I was evaluated annually and rank ordered in relation to my peers. I worked hard at my profession, but so did my peers. I wanted to do my best, but I didn't feel I had to act competitively toward the others. I always wanted them to do well and succeed. I didn't try to "beat" them or put them down. It was an issue of my attitude and my spirit.

To compete in many arenas of life, preparation, hard work, practice, and education are important. We should all augment our natural abilities and gifts. Yet we'll always find others who are better than we are in some skills and abilities. We shouldn't envy them; we should learn from them.

You may be thinking, *But I want to be competitive in my profession so I'll advance and get promoted.* That's a slightly different slant on the word *competitive.* I practice handball so I'll be competitive in my game, but my focus is on my preparation and development, not on simply beating someone else.

Some of us by nature are competitive people. We want to win at all costs. We want to be the best. We're determined to be on the top of the pile. That leads to aggressive behavior and relationships that are more combat than competition. No one likes to be around someone like that — someone who's always "in the game," trying to be superior to everyone around him. Those around him end up hoping he'll fail and fall flat on his face. By contrast, a person who works hard, is gifted, and does well without a sense of crushing the other person will win great respect.

Good leaders will always seek out people who are more gifted and skilled than they are to better the team or the company. They're not threatened by someone who will eventually replace them. They cheer them on rather than see them as competition. I've seen people in my profession of astronautics who are far more gifted than I. They were inspirations, not competition. They didn't slow down my success because they were valued members of the team.

Forget about trying to outshine or outclass others. Just develop yourself and you'll compete well enough without being a self-serving, overly competitive person.

Avoid Pride and Boastfulness

My favorite sport is handball. I enjoy the competition of playing hard to win the game. But no matter how much I practice, my natural athletic limitations often keep me from winning. My opponent's superb athletic coordination gives him the edge over me. I also know people whose intellectual knowledge is superior to mine, and others whose mechanical skills or artistic abilities far surpass mine. Seeing them in action, I think, *What a wonderful gift!* It's a pleasure to see men and women using their God-given talents to the full.

On the other hand, I know there are areas in which I have abilities others don't have.

In either case, should I feel inferior or superior?

I must avoid two hazards: (1) lamenting over my lack or deficiency in skills by comparing myself with others, and (2) being proud or boastful of my skills, accomplishments, and knowledge in those areas in which I excel.

It's easy to become proud of our gifts and look down on those less capable, or to be impatient with someone who doesn't think as quickly or deeply or analytically as we do, or to be frustrated when others don't see things from our perspectives. There's also the danger of believing we deserve all the credit for whatever success we attain. Conversely, at times we might be tempted to feel inferior because we lack the skill or ability we see in another person.

Who gave us our minds and our natural abilities? God did. So who are we to boast, either outwardly or in our hearts? As the apostle Paul said in the New Testament, "What do you have that you did not receive? And if you did receive it, why do you boast as though you did not?"[23] Pride is one of the worst of human flaws, but genuine humility recognizes that God is the giver of "every good and perfect gift."[24]

We can be pleased with our success and accomplishments without being prideful. We can enjoy them without boasting. And we can use our gifts to the fullest without thinking less of someone else who doesn't match our level of achievement.

What then is our responsibility? We must develop our God-given gifts by whatever means we can: education, practice, focus, and training. But all the while, we're to recognize that we're stewards, not owners, of our gifts and capabilities.

Some of our gifts will diminish with age, poor health, or injury. But we must not allow them to deteriorate through lack of use, inflexibility, or failure to grow. The same applies to whatever wealth or opportunities we have. We can't take credit for earning them, but we're responsible for using them well.

So take pleasure in your gifts while also openly rejoicing in the gifts of others. As a special and unique creation, acknowledge that you're the recipient of many gifts. Do this openly, especially in your heart.

49

DO WHAT YOU SAY YOU'LL DO

During my last senior responsibility in the Air Force Reserves, I had about a dozen colonels and generals working directly for me (working *with* me, in many respects, since they reported to other active-duty commanders). All of us were reservists who held significant responsibilities in the civilian world—as company presidents, government executives, engineers, and other professionals. We all led busy lives.

In my first meeting with them, I shared my vision and values guiding our joint responsibility for about 2,500 reservists on ten military bases. I said, "Through the years, I've come to understand the importance of one value: If you say you'll do something, then I shouldn't have to check on it again. If you cannot do it, just let me know. If you don't have the time or resources to do it, let me know. Otherwise I'll assume the responsibility is being carried out."

To some, that may sound harsh or demanding. Yet through

the years, both in military and civilian work, I've found that keeping my word and doing what I said I would do gained me more respect than my skill or ability, as skill and ability are of little use when not applied in a dependable way.

I also remember occasions when I told my own supervisors that I was unable to do a task, either within the time allotted or with the resources I had.

Why is this habit of life so important?

- It marks you as a person of your word.
- It makes you a load lifter on your team.
- It makes you a more valuable employee.
- It honors your coworkers.
- It's the right thing to do.

People who do what they promise to are usually sought out, appreciated, and eventually honored.

But consider how you would be regarded if you *didn't* do what you said you'd do. You would be called undependable, unfaithful, a slacker, a poor worker. Others wouldn't want you on their team; they'd look instead for someone they could count on.

Through the years, I've been privileged to work with a great number of people who are brilliant, skilled, creative, hardworking, and resourceful. I appreciate these qualities, but given the basis of honesty and integrity, I value most that people do what they say they'll do.

Horton the elephant said it well in Dr. Seuss's *Horton Hatches the Egg*: "I meant what I said and I said what I meant. An elephant's faithful, one hundred percent!" And Solomon said, "Reliable friends who do what they say are like cool drinks in sweltering heat—refreshing!"[25]

Expect Your Leaders to Disappoint You

We know instinctively that nobody's perfect. But somehow, when it comes to leaders, we expect them to be virtually perfect. We want them to be visionaries, pioneers, innovators, good managers, and positive role models in every area. We expect them to have razor-sharp judgment, unlimited energy and patience, exemplary families, and faultless morals—plus be available to us 24/7.

Okay, that may be a bit overstated. Yet at the first hint of weakness or failure in a leader, many of us too easily begin to criticize.

Under scrutiny like this, no wonder some of us don't want to lead. We shouldn't be surprised that many leaders who do take the risk and are "found wanting" end up leaving discouraged and disheartened.

The reality is that each one of us—including every leader, and including you and me—has weaknesses. We all have areas where we're not gifted and never will be. We all experience vulnerability, error, insecurity, and pride, and no leader is immune to that. It's true: nobody's perfect.

Yet I've wondered why the effectiveness of some leaders is so quickly hindered by their weaknesses. Perhaps it's the result of how they came to be in leadership roles in the first place — they were the only ones available or they "earned" the positions only by seniority. They may have been thrust into their roles with little preparation for leadership and with even less development afterward.

Sometimes leaders have the competency to lead but lack the character that followers long for. And while efforts continue to further develop leadership skills and competence, development of the leader's character is often neglected.

Whatever the cause, when a leader's weaknesses begin to show, we can become disappointed and start criticizing. But there are constructive ways to counter our critical impulses. We can help make our leaders successful by being tolerant and understanding of their natural weaknesses. If we have issues with a leader, we should make sure we bring it up with him or her before talking about it to others.

And what about our disappointment with *ourselves* as leaders? We can disappoint ourselves when we see subtle or glaring flaws in our character or realize our lack of giftedness in a needed area. Sometimes we expect more of ourselves than we can hope to deliver. Sometimes we exhibit poor judgment and make wrong decisions, and people get hurt or marginalized. Some of us find it so difficult to admit our weaknesses and mistakes as leaders; others of us see our own frailties all too well and are harshly self-critical.

It helps for a leader to understand his limits and to work with others as a team. Don't cling to a leadership role; you may have more lasting influence without it! And admit when your job as a leader is done. Always show others that you value them and the organization above your private needs.

Above all, we need to extend grace both to others and to ourselves. Grace is needed by every leader as well as every follower—after all, nobody's perfect.

51 Learn in Depth — Don't Be Shallow

When you're choosing a physician, an auto mechanic, or a computer technician, what kind of person do you look for? Not someone who's mediocre, but a tried-and-true expert who really knows his or her profession.

It's important to know our specific gifts, talents, and abilities and not try to be an expert in everything. Once we know what we can and should be doing, we can do it best by following this principle: *Learn thoroughly and in depth—don't be shallow.*

I developed this conviction after realizing that my early tendency to do too many things resulted in my becoming "a mile wide and an inch deep."

I've seen the importance of this in-depth approach in many ways. When a new office building was being constructed for the organization I work for, the site chosen was on a sloping hill. A hole was dug that was eighteen feet deep, and wider and longer than the building would be. In that hole, the builders placed a system of drains installed for groundwater runoff and covered it with alternating layers of clay and a granular fill, creating a level base for pouring the concrete foundation. All this before any part of the building appeared above ground!

In my profession of astronautics, I soon found I couldn't just "get by"; I had to work hard to become an expert in specific aspects of my specialty. At age twenty-four, I was working as a space mission controller at Cape Canaveral in the early days of America's space program. Every time I got into technical discussions, I realized how little I knew and how I needed to grow technically. My fellow controllers all had master's degrees, so I was encouraged to go back to graduate school for two grueling years of study.

Let me urge you to go deep in a few selected areas. Learn more about your job, and be the best you can be. Attend professional conventions and learn from your peers. Take time to go deep. Do what you do with excellence.

If you're a parent, read parenting books and go to parenting seminars. As a husband or wife, learn how to grow in your marriage relationship. In the spiritual areas, be serious about discovering what you truly believe and allow it to affect your life in practical ways.

52 FINISH

Don't be a quitter. If you've been entrusted with a task, see it through to the end.

I've had a standard speech for those who worked for me. "If you say you'll do something, I need to know you'll do it. If you can't do it, please tell me. If you don't know how to do it, ask for help. But, please, don't say you'll do something and then not do it."

This is an issue of both faithfulness and dependability. People don't get kudos for what they start, only for what they finish. Many inventors set out to create a lightbulb, but today we remember only the name of the man who went all the way: Thomas Edison.

Finishing is different from winning. In the 1968 Olympics in Mexico City, athlete John Stephen Akhwari represented Tanzania in the marathon. A fall during the race gave him a badly cut knee and dislocated the joint, but he got back to his feet and kept going. Hobbled by the injury, he finished last in the event, far behind the other competitors. When asked why he didn't simply withdraw from the race, he replied, "My country did not send me to Mexico City to start the race. They sent me to finish."

I'm not particularly adept with my hands (except in handball!). I remember struggling with projects in woodworking class in high school, being not particularly skilled at it. But the teacher made me finish my projects. I still have a wooden lamp that I made, and I'm proud of having finished it. There's a satisfaction in completing something.

When you have a reputation of being a finisher, you'll earn great freedom and respect. Be a finisher and you'll discover a world of opportunity opening to you.

Notes

1. (Romans 12:3, NLT).
2. (Isaiah 51:1).
3. (Ephesians 4:26, NASB).
4. (Psalm 102:17).
5. (Philippians 4:6).
6. (verse 7).
7. (Deuteronomy 8:18).
8. (Proverbs 11:24-25, NLT).
9. (Proverbs 5:3-4,7-9, MSG).
10. (verse 6, MSG).
11. Gordon MacDonald, *Ordering Your Private World* (Nashville: Thomas Nelson, 2003), 141.
12. (Luke 6:31).
13. (Luke 10:27).
14. (Romans 12:16, MSG).
15. (Proverbs 15:1,4, MSG).
16. (Luke 16:10, NASB).
17. (Romans 12:18).
18. (Proverbs 18:24).

19. (1 Corinthians 13:4-8, MSG).
20. (Proverbs 14:23).
21. (Proverbs 6:6-11, MSG).
22. (Matthew 20:26-27).
23. (1 Corinthians 4:7).
24. (James 1:17).
25. (Proverbs 25:13, MSG).

About the Author

JERRY WHITE, international president emeritus of The Navigators, is a popular speaker at conferences and seminars. He received a bachelor of science in electrical engineering from the University of Washington and a PhD in astronautics from Purdue University. Dr. White served as a mission controller at Cape Canaveral, was an associate professor at the U.S. Air Force Academy, and retired from the Air Force in 1997 as a major general.

He is the author of several books, including *The Joseph Road*; *Honesty, Morality, and Conscience*; *Dangers Men Face*; and *Making Peace with Reality*.

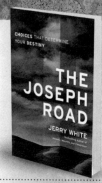
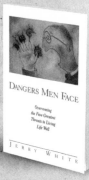
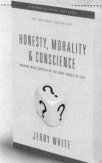